Classic Wood Finishing

George Frank
Revised by Sam Allen

Sterling Publishing Co., Inc.
New York

DEDICATION
To All Fine Finishers

Library of Congress Cataloging-in-Publication Data

Frank, George, 1903–
Wood finishing with George Frank.

Includes index.
1. Wood finishing. I. Title.
TT325.F655 1988 684.1'043 87-26758
ISBN 0-8069-6562-2

10 9 8 7 6 5 4 3 2 1

Published by Sterling Publishing Company, Inc.
387 Park Avenue South, New York, New York 10016
The original edition of this book was published
under the title *Wood Finishing with George Frank*

Distributed in Canada by Sterling Publishing
℅ Canadian Manda Group, One Atlantic Avenue, Suite 105
Toronto, Ontario, Canada M6K 3E7
Distributed in Great Britain and Europe by Cassell PLC
Wellington House, 125 Strand, London WC2R 0BB, England
Distributed in Australia by Capricorn Link (Australia) Pty Ltd.
P.O. Box 6651, Baulkham Hills, Business Centre, NSW 2153, Australia
Printed in Hong Kong

Sterling ISBN 0-8069-7063-4

Contents

Introduction by Sam Allen

As someone who has been involved in woodworking since I was a teenager and who has studied and written books on wood finishing, I have come to recognize the profound effect George Frank has had on this craft. When I studied wood finishing, the innovations of Frank had become so firmly established that they were taught as standard wood-finishing techniques, without any credit given to the man. As you will read in the chapter "Milestones in Wood Finishing," Frank laments that several techniques he patented were imitated by others before the ink on the patents was dry.

It wasn't until I began doing independent research on wood finishing that I found out what a debt of gratitude we owe George Frank. He was truly one of the innovators of twentieth-century wood finishing. He was also a link to the traditional techniques, passing them on to a new generation of wood finishers. His efforts have helped to elevate wood finishing to the high level it enjoys today.

Frank was born on September 16, 1903, in Mako, Hungary. He studied wood finishing at the Kass Guyla Institute in Budapest. After graduating, he found that there was little work in post–World War One Hungary, so he moved to Paris, France, in 1924.

It was in Paris that his creative talent blossomed. Paris in the 1920s was a Mecca for Art Deco design. He quickly found work in a large architectural woodworking plant, where he developed new finishing techniques and refined old ones to complement the Art Deco furniture of the period. After much experimentation, he prepared fifteen samples of finishes he had developed, and used them to win a foreman's job at Jansen, considered the most prestigious woodworking establishment in Paris. After several years at Jansen, he opened his own finishing business, which quickly became the premier finishing establishment in the French capital.

George Frank was responsible for transforming wood finishing from a lowly craft to a highly regarded art. He was fond of telling others that when he first arrived in Paris he and his fellow finishers were required to eat at a separate table at restaurants because no one wanted to associate with them. Within only a few years, however, he was asked by an ex-prince to honor his table.

In 1939, Frank moved to New York and established his wood-finishing business, the George Frank Cabinet Corporation, in Manhattan. In 1978, he retired and moved to Florida, but he continued to experiment with wood finishes throughout his life. During his later years, he shared his knowledge through seminars, articles, and books. He died on September 2, 1997.

I am honored that Sterling Publishing Company has asked me to revise this landmark finishing book. I have not deleted any of the original material. Instead, I have expanded on some of Frank's information. In several cases, he predicted changes that would be significant to the future of finishing. Those predictions have come true, and in those cases I have updated the reader concerning these changes.

Sam Allen

Sam Allen has been involved with woodworking for over thirty years. He has worked in custom and mass-production cabinet and furniture shops. He apprenticed with several experienced woodworkers and studied wordworking at Brigham Young University, College of Industrial and Technical Education. There he experimented with little-used traditional and new finishing techniques. He is the author of several woodworking books, including *Wood Finisher's Handbook*, *Finishing Basics*, and *Classic Finishing Techniques*.

Preface

One of my favorite books is *Colas Breugnon*, by Romain Rolland—the story of a woodworker who lived about two hundred years ago in the Burgundy region of France. A robust fellow, he not only accepted life's challenges, he also enjoyed coping with them. He was the ideal woodworker—one who used his brain, his brawn, and his heart.

Two hundred years ago, if a woodworker like Breugnon wanted to build a cabinet, he had to go to the forest, select and cut down one or two trees, make lumber of them, dry the lumber, build the cabinet, carve the area decorations (if carving were involved), and then do his own woodturning, shaping, bending, inlay work, and, of course, finishing.

Woodworking has changed drastically during the past two hundred years. It has been broken down into many specialized subtrades. Lumber is bought at the lumberyard, the woodturner does the turnings, the carver the carving, and the finishing is now entrusted to the specialized wood finisher.

When I entered the trade over sixty years ago, I was ashamed to reveal that I was a wood finisher. Today I am proud to be one. The profession has grown in leaps and bounds in the interim and is now accorded the respect it deserves.

Not only is wood finishing now accepted as a trade, it is rapidly becoming a science and an art. And, while the youngest among woodworking subtrades, it already has two different factions: those providing for production finishing and those favoring fine finishing.*

Today we have government-financed schools that teach fine wood finishing. We also have an official publication, *The Wood Finisher*,

*Though a rich language, English falls short when it comes to words that distinguish differences in quality in the woodworking trades. For example, the German word *Kunsttischler* refers exclusively to refined, advanced, or artistic workers in the cabinetmaking trade. I am trying to achieve the same distinction when I combine the adjective "fine" with finisher or finishing.

the first one in the world written by wood finishers for wood finishers. In the planning stage is a government-financed testing laboratory and, by the time you read this book, there could very well be an association of wood finishers.

As someone who has grown with my profession, I have become involved in some of the major breakthroughs in wood finishing. Now I want to share this knowledge and experience with you.

Years ago, I visited a shipyard in Germany and watched a machine used to knock rust and paint off ships. The machine resembled hundreds of cold chisels hitting the hull alternately with great speed and force. My mind being what it was, I was convinced that I was on the verge of discovering a new wood-finishing technique. I returned the next day with a few one-inch-thick boards and a bottle of schnapps (a gift for the worker operating the machine in return for his cooperation).

The worker tried his machine on the boards. The experiment was a failure (the only thing I discovered was another way to manufacture toothpicks). But it was a worthwhile attempt, because the key to wood finishing is experimentation. During my years in the trade, I was never satisfied with routine accomplishments, and through experimentation always tried to improve my finishing techniques.

The future of wood finishing is in your hands. Take the information I am presenting here and use it in your workshop. Never stop experimenting, and don't be afraid of failure. Occasional failure and the thrill of success are all part of the heritage that wood finishers share.

George Frank lecturing at the Academy of Wood Technology, in Budapest, from which he graduated.

Safety Procedures

Woodworking, when performed with the proper care, is not very hazardous; wood finishing, when done with the proper care, can be even less hazardous. I have practised wood finishing in my shops for over sixty years, and have had very few accidents.

My contention that wood finishing is one of the safest of the woodworking trades is sustained not only by the low insurance rates for wood finishers, as compared to other craftsmen in the woodworking field, but also by a look at the most recent and most complete catalogues of finishing items put out by the major suppliers. These catalogues contain very few safety items that can be used in the finishing room. Obviously, there is not a great demand for these items.

Still, the key to performing a wood-finishing job carefully is to be aware of the potential dangers that await you in the finishing room, and the best ways to deal with them. Therefore, it is essential that I point these dangers out to you.

Without any doubt, fire is the greatest hazard. The finisher works with readily flammable ingredients; many of them are actually explosives. Pay attention to all the warnings on the labels, treat the ingredients with due care and respect, and follow the guidelines described below, which I used in my workshops.

In my factory, I stored all my flammable material in a concrete shed outdoors, from where we brought in only the amount needed for that day; this material we kept in spring-closed containers. Of course, smoking was forbidden, and all lights and other electrical equipment had to be spark-proof. Waste was collected in heavy-gauge tin cans with self-closing lids. We stretched a clothesline not far from the back of the room, on which we hung oily rags to dry overnight (otherwise, they might have self-ignited).

At my shop, we had on hand the number of special fire extinguishers required by law. As an added safety precaution, I also had available several gallon pails filled with sand, which is one of the best ways to put out a starting fire.

Throughout my business life I took every possible precaution to prevent fire, and was successful. All these precautions should be applied by you, too. Adapt these guidelines for your own workshop.

The use of chemicals to finish wood is another area of concern. Not all chemicals used by wood finishers are dangerous or poisonous in the particular form they are used in. For example, I use sulfuric acid as a mordant. However, I don't use it in its pure, concentrated form, which is extremely potent. One drop of sulfuric acid on your skin will probably leave a mark for life. Instead, I use vitriol, the commercial version of this acid that contains one part acid for nine parts of water. Accidentally splashing vitriol on yourself can be painful, but if that happens and you wash it off promptly, you can minimize the discomfort.

Wood finishers almost never use acid in its original concentrated form; instead, they use diluted versions of it. There are a few exceptions. I have carried pure undiluted versions of acids like sulfuric, muriatic (hydrochloric), and acetic acid in stock, but I carefully stored them—clearly labelled on the highest shelf in my stockroom—so that no one could reach them by mistake. Furthermore, I wrote on the label for each of them this warning: "Never add water to acid; add acid to water." If water is poured into some acids, a violent reaction may take place that may spray acid out of the container.

Almost all of the chemicals used as a stain or dye are either poisonous, caustic, harmful, or irritating in some way; so use them with caution. Read and follow all warnings listed on the containers.

Don't use poisonous chemicals to finish children's furniture or for items that will come into contact with food. Keep chemicals out of the reach of children. Fumes and vapors caused by these chemicals are another potential hazard. Many wood finishers open a bottle and try to identify its contents by smelling it. Do not do this. The bottle should have a label on it identifying its contents; if that label is missing, you must be very careful. Open the bottle, hold it away from your nose, and, with your free hand, fan the fumes or vapors towards your nose.

To avoid inhaling harmful fumes or dust from chemicals, sanding operations, or the overuse of spray equipment, open all doors and windows to ensure adequate ventilation. Turn on a fan and wear a dust mask or respirator when performing operations that produce dust or fumes.

Eye protection is another important safety consideration. Goggles or a full face shield should be worn whenever caustic or irritating materials are being used.

Finally, if there are sounds in the workshop that distract you, buy a pair of earplugs.

****

The best advice I could give you concerning safety in the workshop comes in the form of a story.

Early in the 1950s I purchased a three-story factory building in the East Harlem section of New York and outfitted it to meet the needs of a medium-size modern woodworking shop, complete with safety devices. It became, and still is, the home of the George Frank Cabinet Corporation.

With a crew of 10 to 15 well-qualified workers, we specialized mostly in architectural woodwork, such as interiors, banks, and showrooms designed by architects or interior decorators. Our first three years in this new location turned out to be highly successful, and at Christmastime I was able to give my workers generous bonuses.

We did not fare as well the fourth year. Within the first six months, there were three accidents in the shop. These accidents were costly in more than one way. They were, of course, costly to the men who were hurt. And they were costly to me because of the lost man-hours and because production slowed down.

At Christmastime that fourth year, I realized that the company had barely made ends meet. In spite of that, I did not forsake the traditional Christmas party in the shop or bonuses for the men. However, the envelopes contained about one-fourth the bonus of the preceding years, and a letter that I can quote from memory:

"My Friends, My Fellow Woodworkers:

"Accidents are costly. The three that happened early this year cost you some extra Christmas money, and me far more. Accidents don't just happen; they are caused by carelessness. No saw leaps out of its shaft to cut your finger. You must feed your finger to the saw.

"We have always had all the safety devices you need. I never rushed you or forced you to bypass using them, yet we have had three accidents. The reason for these accidents is that all three men failed to use the most important safety devices in your shop: *care and consideration.*

"I cannot afford to have careless workers in my shop because they cost too much, and you cannot afford to have careless mates, since they are shrinking your Christmas bonus.

"I will have no sympathy for the next accident victim, and if his accident is a major one, he will have to look for another job when he is healed. So, let's have no more accidents!"

I signed the letter: "Your Boss. More, Your Friend."

The sentiments expressed in my letter may have seemed harsh, but they were accurate and they focused my workers' thoughts on the importance of being aware and careful at all times.

And it worked! For the following eighteen years, during which time I owned the corporation, there was not a single major accident and only a few minor ones—and we had eighteen rousing Christmas parties!

Accept the advice of someone who has had firsthand experience. Use care and concentration. Don't wait until you have had an accident in your workshop. Always make safety your *first* priority.

Why Finish Wood?

There are basically two reasons for finishing wood: to protect it or to beautify it. In this book, I will explain finishing methods in which either or both concerns are addressed.

Protecting Wood

Wood has three natural enemies: fire, water (moisture), and decay-causing microbes (fungi) or insects. Man, a fourth enemy, is the worst, because he sets fire to forests and destroys jungles in his attempts to spread civilization. (Perhaps it is unfair to generalize this severely, for there are those who are sincerely concerned about this resource.)

To some extent, man has found ways to make wood incombustible. "Fireproof" wood, in my opinion, is far more costly, in more ways than one, than the protection it offers is worth. "Fireproof" wood may not burn, but its smoke can be just as lethal. Working with such wood is difficult. It requires carbide-tipped tools and dust masks, which cannot effectively prevent the woodworker from inhaling the noxious dust. Also, although fireproof lumber may be easily available in construction grade, choice cabinet-grade lumber that is fireproof is almost impossible to purchase.

There are additional problems. Even if you are able to buy fireproof solid lumber, you cannot find matching plywood because only the core of the plywood is fireproof; the face veneer is not. Matching the color of the two is virtually impossible; there is only one way, and that is to paint the whole thing shocking pink, preferably with two heavy coats.

I do not advocate the use of fireproof wood, and feel that the best protection against fire, besides the precautions outlined on pages 10 and 11, is to simply use extreme caution.

Water (moisture) is another great enemy of wood. When wood

absorbs moisture from the air, its size increases. When it releases moisture (because of heat and dryness), it shrinks.

One of the more baffling mysteries of nature is the fact that wood apparently keeps "breathing" centuries after it has been made into lumber. Though a tree has been felled, and has been reduced to fractions of its original size, these fractions are still able to change their dimensions and weight through the absorption or release of water. Perhaps this is an indication that in some way or form the tree is still alive.

Woodworkers are constantly engaged in a battle to prevent the increase or decrease in the dimensions of wrought wood. This is not easy to do, and is further complicated by the fact that wood that absorbs moisture enlarges only in the area where the moisture is absorbed—for example, in the top, bottom, or side of the wood. In other words, the wood warps.

Consider the following example: On top of a soaking-wet newspaper, place a ¼-inch-thick solid pine board that's about 8 inches square. The board, perfectly straight at the beginning, will within 20–30 minutes assume a convex shape. This is because the side that was in contact with the wet paper absorbed much moisture from the paper and expanded in size, while the other side remained at its original size.

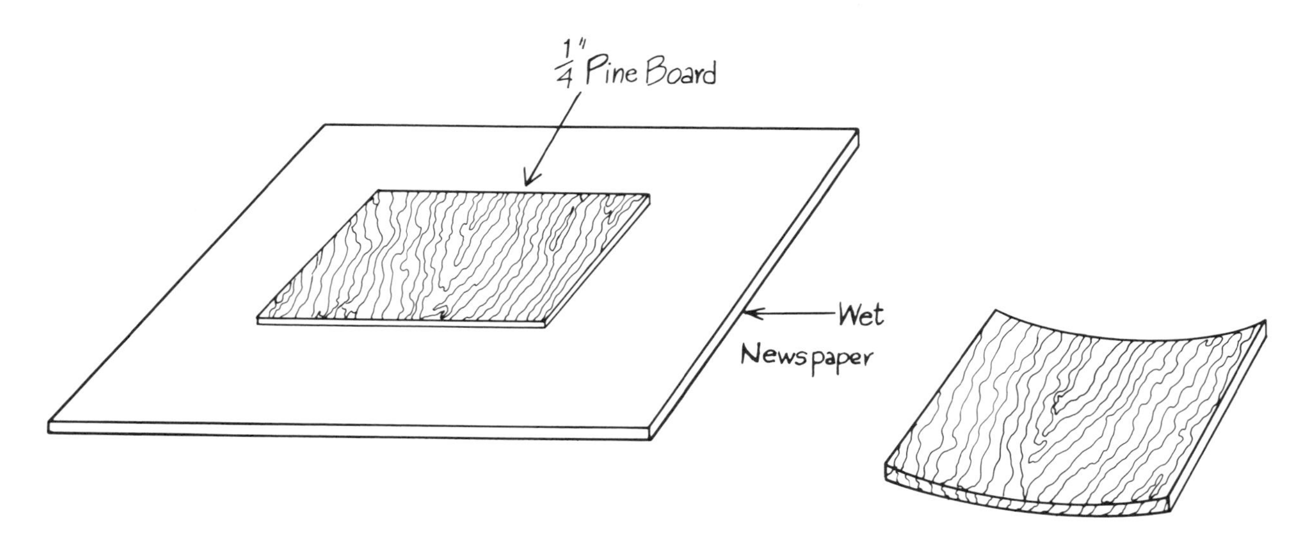

An example of what happens to wood when it absorbs moisture. Top shows ¼-inch board that has been placed on wet newspaper. Note the shape the board assumes 20–30 minutes later.

The lumber-producing industries offer several solutions to this problem. One is the universally accepted plywood that resists moisture absorption or release better than solid wood. Another is the scientifically controlled kiln-drying of wood.

There may be other solutions as well. Almost thirty years ago, a salesman from the U.S. Plywood Company showed me a sample of veneer-core plywood; the glue had been replaced with either plastic or phenolic resin. Though the face wood retained its classical, original markings, and the cross section clearly showed each layer of veneer compounding the core, the whole sample was soaked through—impregnated with colorless plastic.

For the woodworker to work with such plywood, carbide-tipped cutters, special adhesives, and a whole new technology are needed. Finishing and protection are not required; both are built in. This plywood comes the closest to the dimensionally stable, water-moisture-resistant wood described.

Around the same time, a Japanese friend of the family brought us samples of products from his family's company: plywood handles, knobs, and other objects made of the same plastic laminates. A Japanese company, the Nitta Veneer Manufacturing Co., Ltd., is presently marketing in the United States furniture knobs and handles made of this wood-and-plastic combination under the trade name Complite®.

Wood finishing has played a part in the fight against the problems caused by water moisture. Moisture enters the wood through its pores, which are tiny openings. The finish, whatever it is, will fill or reduce these openings, thus reducing the chances of the moisture entering the wood.

Fungi and bacteria are microscopic organisms of various forms that contribute to the putrefaction, or rotting, of wood. Termites, borers, and other worms are also factors; they simply eat the wood. Science has made great advances in thwarting the effects of decay-causing microbes and insects. For example, the construction industry markets at little extra cost—mainly in the warm or tropical regions—a wood that is treated in such a way that it is unfit as food for insects and resists rot.

The cabinetmaker, on the other hand, is faced with the problem of woodworms, which seem to have a fondness for antiques. During my research on these creatures, I came across a reference to no fewer than 16 species. No less an authority than Daniel Alcouffe, the erudite curator of the Louvre, told me that there is no effective remedy—as yet—against them. Restorers in the Louvre are experimenting with two insecticides, "Xylamone" and "Xylophene," both commercial products; they either apply them with a brush or inject them into the wormholes with a hypodermic needle. Though these insecticides may kill the bugs they can reach, they may also affect the color of the wood and its finish. Other restorers are experimenting with strong-smelling formaldehyde; it's applied in the same way as the insecticides, with the same limited success.

I learned from one who repairs and restores antiques for the Museum of Industrial Art in Budapest that borers are sensitive to temperature changes, and can be killed by both heat and cold; my own experiments later on confirmed his findings.

There is a tendency in America to hold imported wood-preserving products in higher esteem than domestic ones. This does a great disservice to American products and technology. One American company, the Ventron Corporation, markets a wide variety of fungicides, wood preservatives, and antimicrobials for the wood industries.

Three potentially devastating weapons against boring insects may appear in the near future: gamma rays, ultrasonic sounds, and microwaves. Experiments with gamma rays already appear to be successful.

Stains, Dyes, and Chemical Treatments

The fine wood finisher not only fights against the enemies of wood, he also strives to find ways to enhance its beauty. Ways of enhancing the beauty of wood are: changing the color of the wood, changing its tactile quality, and emphasizing its markings. The three basic ways to change the color of wood are through staining, dyeing, or treating with chemicals.

Stains

Knowing and understanding the differences between stains and dyes is the first requisite for understanding wood finishing. Here is what was written in the *Cabinetmaker's Guide*—a book printed over a hundred and sixty years ago in London, England: "Staining differs from the process of dyeing inasmuch as it penetrates just below the surface of the wood, instead of colouring its substance throughout."

Three basic ingredients found in every stain, paint, or filler are pigments, carriers, and binders. Pigment is basically any solid object that can be reduced into powder. For example, if you break up in a mortar a piece of chalk you'll have white pigment, called whiting.

While travelling in Colorado, I picked up a handful of red earth, dried it completely in an oven, pulverized it, and strained it. As a result, I produced the same type of pigment Americans are importing from Italy (and paying too much money for): the sienna colors (burnt or raw sienna).

Pigments are colored matter used to impart their colors to other materials. However, pigments alone cannot do this. For example, with the powder from my Colorado earth we can cover a board of wood; this board will look red as long as we don't shake the powder off it or a wind blows away the powder. Another substance is needed to hold the particles of the pigment together and fasten them to the board of wood. This essential substance is called the *binder*. Suppose, for example, that prior to spreading the red powder on the board, we cover it with glue. The glue (binder) will adhere to the board and hold the red powder so well that it cannot be shaken or blown off.

Let's add another element to this example. We can mix the red powder and the glue together. We thin the glue in the mixture with water, which makes it easier to spread and ensures that there is an even application of the mixture. The water, which is the *carrier* or *solvent*, evaporates fairly fast. Until it does, the wood coated with the mixture will be red and tacky. When the water evaporates, the color will be permanently attached to the wood.

Let's look at two more examples. Suppose the red powder from Colorado is mixed with spar varnish (a binder, when it dries). The varnish will turn red (the color of the pigment), and the mixture becomes heavy and difficult to spread. When turpentine (carrier) is added, the mixture is far easier to work with; this mixture is now a paint. It covers the board and, regardless of the color of the wood, imparts the color of the *pigment* to the board.

In our next example, suppose the powdered red earth from Colorado is mixed with turpentine; this produces a red, milklike liquid of about medium consistency. Next, we add varnish sparingly to it. The result is a very thin coating, not heavy enough to cover or hide the wood, but still strong enough to convey much of its color to it. Such a mixture is no longer a paint; it is now a stain. This stain consists of a pigment (pulverized red earth), a binder (varnish, reduced), and a carrier (turpentine) that makes the application of the stain on the wood easier.

Stains will not penetrate the wood, even if they are applied liberally. The pigment can enter the microscopic openings of the wood, and will eventually alter the color of the wood, but will *never* change it.

Stains can really be considered thinned-down paints, and as such they obscure the natural graining of the wood—which is the reason fine finishers do not like to use them. A fine finisher wants to "read" the wood and enjoy the beauty of its markings; therefore, he uses dyes.

Universal Colors

Cans or tubes of Universal colors can be purchased at paint suppliers. They are simply pigments reduced to very fine powder; this fine powder is then mixed with a carrier, probably mineral spirit or mineral oil. It is marketed ready to be mixed into stains, paints, waxes, or fillers.

There is an interesting relationship between finishing oils and waxes, their solvents. Waxes, when heated, become liquid and can easily be dissolved in mineral spirit, turpentine, gasoline, or even lacquer thinner. Oils can be thinned with these same solvents. Before dissolving melted wax in mineral spirit, it is possible to dissolve dye in it; the result will be coloring wax. Mixing colored pigments in it will add to the coloring power of the wax or waxes.

Dyes

The 1825 issue of the *Cabinetmaker's Guide* contains the following description of how to produce "fine black" dye: "Have a chair-maker's copper fixed, into which put six pounds of chip logwood, and as many veneers as it will conveniently hold, without pressing too tight; fill it with water and let it boil slowly for about three hours; then add half a pound of powdered verdigris, half a pound of copperas, and four ounces of bruised nutgalls, filling the copper up with vinegar, as the water evaporates; let it boil gently two hours each day, till you find the wood to be dyed through; which, according to the kind, will be in more or less time."

The tradesman who wrote these lines more than a hundred and sixty years ago realized that when the white sycamore veneer was cooked in the brew described, it became black throughout. He also realized that not all wood or veneers must be boiled or cooked for hours and hours; dyes can be applied much like stains on the finished product. In his description, he underlined clearly the basic difference between stains and dyes: "Dyes will change the color of the wood, while stains cover the wood with a thin layer of coloring matter."

Today, dye and pigment manufacturing, based on extensive scientific research, has become a huge, worldwide industry. In 1980, the world produced about one million tons of dyes and pigments. A great deal of printed matter on the subject is available, yet very few publications concerning the dyeing of wood contain clear, concise information. It is my belief that the following information and historical background will help to clarify how and why dyes are used.

Old Dyes

Old dyes have a fascinating background. Dyes were used in China three thousand years ago. Dyed objects from as far back as forty-five hundred years ago have been excavated in India. Dyed mummy wrapping dating back to 2,000 B.C. has been found in Egypt.

There are abundant records concerning these dyes. We know where they come from, what they can do, and how to use them. We even know about the people who used them.

Throughout history, dyes have been used not only to color textiles, but also in a social context. In the Bible, Moses was instructed to accept gifts of "blue and purple and scarlet and fine linen and goat's hair." In Rome during the reign of the Caesars, those who used the color Tyrian Purple without authorization were severely punished. (Tyrian Purple is also called Cardinal Red because at another time it was reserved only for political or church leaders like the cardinals.) During the Elizabethan period in England, it was against the law to use indigo and logwood in woodworking shops.

There are also legends and superstitions associated with some of the plants from which the dyes are produced. A root named mandrake produces a yellow dye. Mandrake belongs to a potato-tuber family that grows mostly around the Mediterranean and in the Orient. Its roots resemble the carrot's, but are rather hairy and split in two just like human legs. The plant itself grows in the shadows of trees.

Perhaps because of the way the plant looks or the way it grows, supernatural powers have been associated with it. Among the mystical powers attributed to it: It makes its holder invisible and protects him or her from witchcraft, sickness, and even lawsuits; it also ensures easy conceptions and childbirths for women.

THE ÉBÉNISTES

Gilles Gobelin, who was Scandinavian, immigrated to France during the 15th century and opened up a textile-dyeing factory in Paris's *rue Mouffetard*. There Gilles brazenly challenged the Italians, accepted masters of the textile-dyeing art, and soon earned a reputation as a *fou* (madman).

But Gilles was anything but crazy. In his factory—called by some "Gobelin's Folly"—he reproduced the Tyrian Purple at a fraction of the price the Italians charged for it.

The Gobelins' factory deservedly grew in size and reputation. The government, under Louis XIV, eventually took it over and it became the *Manufacture Royale des Meubles de la Couronne*, the factory where most of the masterpieces of the period were created, and also where master woodworkers, the *ébénistes*, worked side by side with the textile dyers.

There is little doubt in my mind that this is where the art of dyeing wood originated.

Through their simple experiments with dyes used on textiles, our trade ancestors produced colors that even today have not been surpassed. Following is a discussion of some of these dyes.

LOGWOOD, BRAZILWOOD, AND YELLOWWOOD

About one hundred and fifty years ago, chips from three different woods were used frequently for dye-making. These woods were logwood (*Haematoxylon campechianum*), brazilwood (*Caesalpinia bahamensis*), and yellowwood (*Cladrastis lutea*).

Logwood is probably the most popular of the old dyes. It is easily available, potent, versatile, and produces exciting colors. Both the chips from yellowwood and the powdered extract can produce an array of yellows, browns, and olive colors.

Brazilwood has an interesting history. As already mentioned, dyes were extracted from plants as early as three thousand years ago. One such plant, the *Caesalpinia l.*, was identified and named after Italian naturalist Andrea Caesalpino in the 16th century. He studied this evergreen and discovered that it belonged to a family of approximately 40 plants that thrive in warm climates. A large tree of this family, the *Caesalpinia brasiliensis*, which grew to a height of 20 to 25 feet, had been noted by 14th-century herbalists for both its coloring and curative properties. Until the advent of synthetic dyes, the extract from this tree, which grew mainly in the Bahamas, was a mainstay among red dyes. The best source for these extracts was the *Caesalpinia pernambuci*. Approximately half-a-dozen members of the *Caesalpinia* family, such as the *bijuga*, *karangua*, and *crista* trees, were known for their color-producing qualities. They all produced the precious dye known as *brazilein*.

Strangely enough, when South America was discovered in 1500, the early prospectors soon noticed an abundance of such trees and called it the "Land of the Brazilein"—Brazil. Today, brazilein is still a magnificent dye in the hands of the fine finisher. It is easily available under the name of brazilwood extract. Like logwood, brazilwood extract is powerful and versatile. With the proper mordants, it can produce stunning reds and purples and all shades of these colors.

BROU DE NOIX

Another old dye is the classic *brou de noix*, or walnut brew, which is replaced or imitated today with walnut crystals or Cassel extract. As an apprentice, I frequently watched my boss's wife make up this simple brew. While on the tree, the hard shell of the walnut is covered with a green hull that falls away from the ripe fruit. This green hull produced walnut brew, which was probably the earliest dye used on wood. Left on the ground, the hull turned brown, and then nearly black. The boss's wife filled a three- or four-gallon earthen crock with the blackened hulls, covered them with water, and brewed them on the kitchen stove over slow heat for three or four days. On the top of the kitchen cupboard she kept, well out of reach, another earthen crock of lye or soda ash (mostly used as a homemade variation of lye). She put a spoonful of this chemical into the walnut brew; neither of us knew at the time that the lye was acting as a mordant. Then she filtered the brew through some cloth, bottled it, corked it tightly, and stored the bottles in the cellar. She had inexpensively produced more than a year's supply of penetrating, walnut-brown dye.

During that same period, the boss's wife kept another earthen crock in the cellar, covered loosely with a wooden lid. The crock was filled halfway with rusty nails, hinges, and scrap iron, which she would cover with vinegar. A week or two later, the vinegar was filtered and bottled; the result was a dye which, when combined with logwood extract, produced a positive black that, when properly cut, had all shades of grey leading to it.

About sixty years later, I tried to duplicate this same process in my shop. I filled a quart-size, screw-top jar halfway with rusty nails, screws, and scrap iron, covered it with vinegar from the kitchen, and tightened the lid on the jar. I promptly forgot about the experiment.

Three weeks later I was entertaining some friends in my home when we heard a loud noise that sounded like a pistol shot coming from my closed shop. I grabbed the key to the shop and, followed by my friends, rushed to investigate. The glass jar containing the iron scrap had exploded. The liquid had splattered all over, dyeing every piece of wood where it had landed; the vinegar had become a potent grey dye. That explosion proved that I had much to learn about chemistry.

INDIGO

Eliah Bennis, a British authority on dyes, wrote in 1815 that "the best dye drug in the world (except the cochineal) is the indigo." A British periodical printed around the same time describes how to use it: "Take a clean glass bottle, into which put one pound of oil of vitriol; then take four ounces of the best indigo, pounded in a mortar into small lumps; put them into the phial (take care to set the bottle into a basin or earthen glazed pan, as it will ferment); after it is quite dissolved, provide an earthen or wooden vessel, so constructed that it will conveniently hold the veneers you mean to dye; fill it rather more than one-third with water, into which pour as much of the vitriol and indigo (stirring it about) as will make a fine blue; which you may know by trying it with a piece of white paper or wood; put in your veneers and let them remain till the dye has struck through."

Indigo was one of the most important dyes of the past, yet it was one that woodworkers failed to accept. There was good reason for that. The dye made from the indigo plant was not easy to produce. The plant had to be crushed, soaked, and fermented, which was altogether too complicated a process.

As a result, indigo has not become popular with those craftsmen who dye wood. However, it is sometimes used by those who dye veneers, and sometimes solids. Near my first shop in Paris in the 1930s was a store called "Sons of the Brothers Delique"; here, dyed veneer was not only sold, the sons took orders to dye veneers to the customer's specifications. Though the owners never revealed how they accomplished this, it is very probable that they, as well as other members of their guild, dyed the veneers following the procedures described by the British craftsman on page 20. They most likely used indigo to produce blue veneers.

Regardless of whether the indigo you bought today is a synthetic dye or has been produced from the indigo plant, it will not perform to your satisfaction unless you combine it with vitriol as a mordant. Use due care when using it in either form. Wear a good pair of rubber gloves.

COCHINEAL

Cochineal is perhaps the best of the old dyes. It is made from the crushed bodies of cochineal insects. The cochineal is a very small insect; it takes 70,000 of them to weigh one pound.

Only the female cochineal is used to make this dye. According to

Dr. Dietrich Shaaf, head of the Entomology Department of the Atlanta Zoo, the male cochineal's mouth is atrophied to complete uselessness. He is born to fulfill one function only: to fertilize the female. He accomplishes that and dies, probably with a smile on his face.

To produce the dye, the finisher would have to reduce the cochineals into powder, then soak the powder in hot water, and finally combine this brew with alum mordant. The result will be colors of exceptional brightness and clear definition.

One interesting historical note about cochineals: They were used to produce the red on the uniforms worn by the British soldiers during the Revolutionary War; these soldiers were known as Redcoats.

MADDER AND CATECHU EXTRACT

Madder root is one of the oldest dye plants. The color extracted from it was used in Egypt and China over four thousand years ago. Extracting the coloring matter of the plant is a complicated process; therefore, use (synthetic) alizarin, which is the coloring chemical of the plant. Alizarin is a versatile dye that produces many shades of high-quality reds and browns.

Alizarin or madder root extract is not hard to find. Either the root or the coloring chemical is acceptable for experimenting.

The experimenting finisher can obtain a wide spectrum of colors ranging from light beige to dark chocolate by combining catechu extract with various mordants. There are two kinds of catechu extract. One comes from the trunk of the catechu tree, grown in eastern India, the other from the leaves of the creeping catechu plant, grown in Indonesia and Ceylon. There is little information on which is better. Both, though, are rich in tannin and can produce attractive colors.

If catechu extract is used as a single dye on any light wood, it conveys a pleasant beige hue. If it is used combined with dichromate of potassium (which acts as a mordant), the ensuing color will be indestructible.

Catechu extract, unlike alizarin or madder root extract, is not easily available.

MISCELLANEOUS DYES

I have just described among hundreds of textile dyes a few that have been adapted for wood-dyeing. Let me add some more rather interesting ones.

Fine antiques acquire with age a golden hue that's hard to define and harder to imitate. However, I found in my wife's kitchen one means to produce this hue: I discovered that a concentrated brew of coffee, chicory, or, best of all, tea, combined with a small amount of picric acid, will convey that golden hue to any reproduction. (I use black-tea brick for making dye.)

Orcanette root adds a welcome reddish hue to French polish. In my shop, I used to soak it in the oil that we used while French-polishing mahogany.

MORDANTS

Mordants are chemicals that fix dyes in materials. In textile-dyeing and wood-dyeing, the mordant is as important an ingredient as the dye. No "old" dye is complete without one.

Following is a list of the most frequently used mordants:

potassium dichromate	tin (stannuous chloride)
copper sulphate	ferrous sulphate
alum	tannic acid
sulfuric acid (vitriol)	muriatic acid
acetic acid (vinegar)	pyrogallic acid
cream of tartar	Glauber's salt

Mordants are rarely added to the dyes. When they are, the color produced seldom equals the quality of the one achieved when they are applied separately. My experience with old dyes indicates, and nearly all instructions specify, that mordants and dyes should be applied alternately on the wood, both as hot as possible. This is a fundamental point in the art of dyeing wood. Both the mordant and dye must penetrate deeply into the fibres of the wood to bring about the wished-for color change.

CHEMICAL TREATMENT OF WOOD

Let's examine a few examples of chemically treating wood. Take a board of solid maple and soak it with a hot solution of tannic acid. When it is dry, lightly sand it; then sponge it again with a hot solution of ferrous sulphate. The wood will turn black promptly, though it may not be a positive black.

Dry the wood, sand it once more, and repeat the operation—logwood first, iron next. This time you will fully assert the black color of the board.

Now, let's look at another example. Take two boards, one maple, the other oak. Soak both with a hot solution of dichromate of potassium. The maple board will accept the color of the solution, a yellow with a reddish hue; the oak will turn rusty red.

There are reasons why the two boards react differently to the solution. Oak wood contains tannic acid. The combination of tannic acid in the wood and the chrome we applied to it produces the pleasant rust color on the oak. The maple doesn't have tannic acid; therefore, there is no chemical reaction. All the dichromate solution does is convey its own color to the maple. If we were to apply a strong solution of tannic acid to the maple board before applying the dichromate solution, it would turn rusty red.

We changed the color of both wood samples through chemical treatment. The chemical solution on the oak acted on another chemical that the wood already contained; the same reaction by the maple was provoked when we introduced the missing chemical into a species of wood that doesn't contain this chemical.

There are many examples of how chemical reactions change the color of wood. During the Napoleonic era, France imported much mahogany wood from Cuba. It was soon discovered that when this wood was treated with dichromate of potassium, its color quality improved greatly. This is what gave the beautiful color to the Empire-period furniture.

The combination of tannic acid and chromium dichromate produces a wide range of browns. The combination of tannic acid and iron compounds produces all shades from pale grey to perfect black.

Ammonia is a gas, although we are more familiar with its watery solution. Ammonia gas can and does change the color of any wood that contains tannic acid, even if the tannic acid has been artificially introduced into that wood. For example, fumed oak is oak that has been exposed to ammonia fumes.

Bleaching

Bleaching is a process that chemically changes the color of wood by *subtracting*, not adding, color from it. We wood finishers have little information about bleaching, and have not really applied to their trade.

We are using only four chemicals to lighten wood; each has its own shortcomings. One of these chemicals, oxalic acid, does a fair job if used correctly, that is, if it is dissolved in hot water without contact with metal. Oxalic acid should be used very warm and very concentrated.

When oxalic acid is used, the residue has to be neutralized. If not neutralized properly, oxalic acid can affect, sometimes badly, the finish applied on top of it. Sandpaper can be used after the oxalic acid dries, but the dust is suffocating. Use a mask!

While others use vinegar to neutralize the residue, I use another very unorthodox method. First, I wash off all the residue I can with clear water, and then I use a half-half solution of commercial Clorox® bleach (a gallon of rainwater to a gallon of Clorox®), making sure that there is good ventilation. The end result is acceptable.

No bleach will perform well unless the wood is clean. "Clean" is a word hard to define when it concerns wood. Though sandpaper usually leaves the wood acceptably clean for most people, it doesn't for me. The wood still contains chemical impurities, which I wash away with a solution of lye, an invaluable aid to the fine finisher. (Lye is not as dangerous as its reputation suggests. You can wash it off your skin with water without any harm being done. And if you work with antiques or the reproductions of antiques, you will soon find out that it is indispensable.)

Usually I dissolve an 8-ounce can of lye in a gallon of water as warm as I can handle it. Wearing gloves, I dissolve the chemical impurities of the areas I intend to bleach with the help of scrubbing brushes. Then I wash off the dirty lye (now carrying the chemical impurities) with plenty of clear water. When I note that my rinsing water is running crystal-clear, I sponge the excess off and let the wood dry. Whatever bleach I will use will do a better job because of this washing.

Of the four bleaching chemicals used in our trade, chlorine was the one that helped me to produce one of the highlights of my career, the colorless color (described on pages 120–122).

Potassium permanganate has been used by some finishers to dye wood to a pleasing brown color. There are better dyes available. The color produced by it fades. I am told that if potassium permanganate is applied to wood and is followed by an application of hyposulfite of sodium (also used by photographers, I believe, to develop negatives), it acts as a bleach.

Bleaching with hydrogen peroxide is rarely practised by the fine finisher, but I'll say a few words here for those who might be tempted to use it. Hydrogen peroxide is the most potent bleach used in the wood-finishing trade. Its power is rated in volumes. The kind I have in my medicine chest is 10 or 12 volume. The kind used for bleaching is 100 or 130 volume.

Hydrogen peroxide bleach is marketed in two bottles. One contains the peroxide, the other lye, or caustic soda.

Hydrogen peroxide not only bleaches wood, it eliminates many of its markings. The bleached wood becomes "characterless," and it is nearly impossible to restore, let alone improve its original beauty.

Hydrogen peroxide spoils easily. It should be kept in clean, dark bottles; if acetamilide (less than 2%), a preservative, is dissolved in it, it will keep longer.

While I had a major role in introducing peroxide bleaching to the wood-finishing trade about fifty years ago, and while peroxide bleaching is a basic part of production-finishing, my advice to the fine wood finisher is don't use it unless you have to. This is because no dye (that I know) will penetrate wood bleached with peroxide, and even if it does it will fail to improve its look. (The word castrate is my favorite description of what peroxide bleach does to wood.) Though oxalic acid and chlorine are not nearly as potent, you must try to get along using them.

The accepted and much-practised way to color and to finish peroxide-bleached wood is to work on it with stains, pigmented finishes, and artificial shadings, and to "distress" it.

Distressing is practised mostly on the production line and, as such, it belongs to the painting-decorating trade. It is used in the reproduction of antiques.

Reproducing pedigreed antiques taxes the craftsman to the fullest of his ability. He must reproduce every detail of the original to perfection, match the colors and the finish of the original, and, on top of all this, copy the wear and tear of the model. I have never attempted such work without having a model to copy; then, if the model had cracks, open joints, dents, bruises, spots, or any other damage on it, I imitated all to the best of my ability. I "distressed" my copy so that it looked like the model. Such distressing requires keen observation and the patience of an angel. My most important rule when doing such work is to never over-distress.

In the preface, I mentioned that though wood finishing is the youngest of the wood trades and has not yet reached its 150th birthday, it has already split into two distinctly different approaches: fine-finishing and production-finishing. Production-finishers today realize that distressing can have a decorative value, and have developed ways to distress that have nothing to do with my methods. Fly specks that I use with great moderation are produced on the assembly line with special spray nozzles. Dents, bruises, scratches, wormholes, and the full gamut of marks achieved through distressing are applied on the unsuspecting piece of furniture, some through the most unorthodox methods. Against all expectations, the final result is actually an acceptable decorative finish.

What I have discussed so far are the basics in your education about natural and old dyes; your real education will only come through practical experience. As a fine finisher, you belong to a circle of craftsmen who share the same interests. Set up a shop with three or four of these craftsmen and do the experimenting together. You can purchase at little expense an arsenal of natural and old dyes, mordants, and a few tools. These experiments will provide you with the indescribable thrill of discovery.

In Paris in the early twenties, we wood finishers were considered lowly craftsmen. Attitudes towards wood finishing have changed. Serious, learned people with inquiring minds are entering the trade. The printing ink will hardly be dry on these pages when new chemicals and techniques will be found to change the color of wood. So far, I've introduced you to the "old-fashioned" ways to change wood's color, using mostly nature-produced dyes. Let's go a step further and review the modern synthetic dyes.

Synthetic Dyes

Sir William Henry Perkins is considered the founder of the aniline dye industry. Born in 1838 to a building contractor, he became one of England's most famous scientists. When Perkins was barely 18, the British colonial empire was being plagued by malaria; the drug to fight it, quinine, was scarce and costly. Perkins's attempt to produce artificial quinine was unsuccessful, but somehow he stumbled upon a dye—the first synthetic dye ever made by man.

Coal tar, from which this dye was made, was not only the base for a host of rich and pleasing colors; today, it is the raw material for drugs, vitamins, explosives, and perfumes. Also, hundreds of synthetics are produced from its derivatives, among them the sweetener saccharin.

While Perkins reaped ample rewards from the discovery, manufacturing, and marketing of the dye, he continued research. About twelve years later, he succeeded in producing synthetic alizarin and was ready to take out a patent on his method. However, a German scientist investigating coal-tar derivatives uncovered the same process and patented it *one day before* Perkins.

There is a lovely French nursery rhyme that has a catchy refrain which goes like this:

"We are the brave carabiniers,
The safeguards of your foyer.
But by unhappy strokes of fate,
We somehow always get there late!"

This, sadly, should be the theme song of the British and American dye industry.

Synthetic dyes (man-made, not nature-made dyes) have been manufactured in Europe and America for the past hundred to hundred-and-thirty years. While I am perhaps not the most competent judge, I don't believe that the American dyes are inferior to the German ones. However, I always seem to buy the German ones, simply because they are better adapted to my needs, or rather to the needs of the wood-finishing industry.

Arti, my German supplier, has produced dyes specially formulated for wood for at least sixty years, and is presently entering the American market. The presentation of their dyes is impeccable. The dye containers are clearly labelled and give easily readable instructions on how to dissolve and use the contents. The same-numbered dye year after year will give you the same satisfying color. Furthermore, lately, a protective plastic sheet (inside the can) proves that the product is factory-sealed and ensures that it has not been tampered with.

Unfortunately, American dyes lack most of these attributes. I am reluctant to repeat their faults one by one, but I can assure you that when the day comes that American dyes come close to or equal the German ones, I will not spend a single penny on the imported ones.

By an unhappy "stroke of fate," American and British dye manufacturers always get there too late. Let's hope that by the time our sluggish dye manufacturers catch up with the industry's German leadership, our present-day synthetic dyes will not be considered obsolete. Wouldn't it be a source of pride for us if a German or Japanese inventor were to try to take out a patent on some newly discovered super-dye, only to discover that an American had beaten him to it the day before?

Incidentally, there is one flaw in Arti's representation of their wood-coloring dyes: They refer to them as "stains." They are not—they do not stain wood, they dye it. I am certain that Arti will soon notice and correct this error.

Also, one more distinction should be noted between Arti dyes and American dyes. I am convinced that the Arti dyes contain some additives acting as a mordant, while American dyes are simply dyes.

TYPES OF SYNTHETIC DYES

Synthetic dyes can be broken down into three categories: water-soluble dyes, alcohol-soluble dyes, and oil-soluble dyes.

The water we use to dissolve our dyes is not the same everywhere. Well water generally is loaded with minerals. City water is frequently loaded with chlorine. I dissolve my dyes in clean rainwater that has no chlorine or minerals in it. If you are as fussy as I am about the quality of the water, use clean rainwater or distilled water.

When alcohol-soluble dyes are discussed, the alcohol referred to is C.D.A.—standard Completely Denatured Alcohol.

I do not have much experience with oil-soluble dyes because I have not had much need for them. However, I decided to do an experiment with them. I put one gram of oil-soluble dye into each of four small containers. Then I poured the same quantity of solvent into each of the containers. I used a different solvent for each container. They were mineral oil, turpentine, gasoline, and lacquer thinner.

Next, I stirred the containers lightly. Five minutes later, I noticed that the lacquer thinner had dissolved all the dye, the gasoline about 80 to 85%, the turpentine about 5 to 10%, and the mineral oil less than 5%, if any.

I then tested the dyeing power of the four solutions. It correlated with their absorption of the dye. The solution with the strongest dyeing power was the lacquer thinner.

This experiment proved one thing: Oil-soluble dyes are not easy to dissolve in oil, but can be easily dissolved in lacquer thinner. Perhaps the term "oil-soluble dye" is an inaccurate one.

Continued on page 81.

Fine finishers seldom use stains, since stains always veil, to some extent, the markings of the wood. In the two stains shown above, water was used as a carrier, rabbit-skin glue as the binder, and whiting, combined with (respectively) raw and burnt sienna, as the pigment. The finish consists of a few coats of shelliq.

Padouk treated with brazilwood and dichromate, and finished with shelliq. The pores of the wood shown on this page and on pages 34, 35, 38–41, and 71 seem to be filled with white filler. They are not.

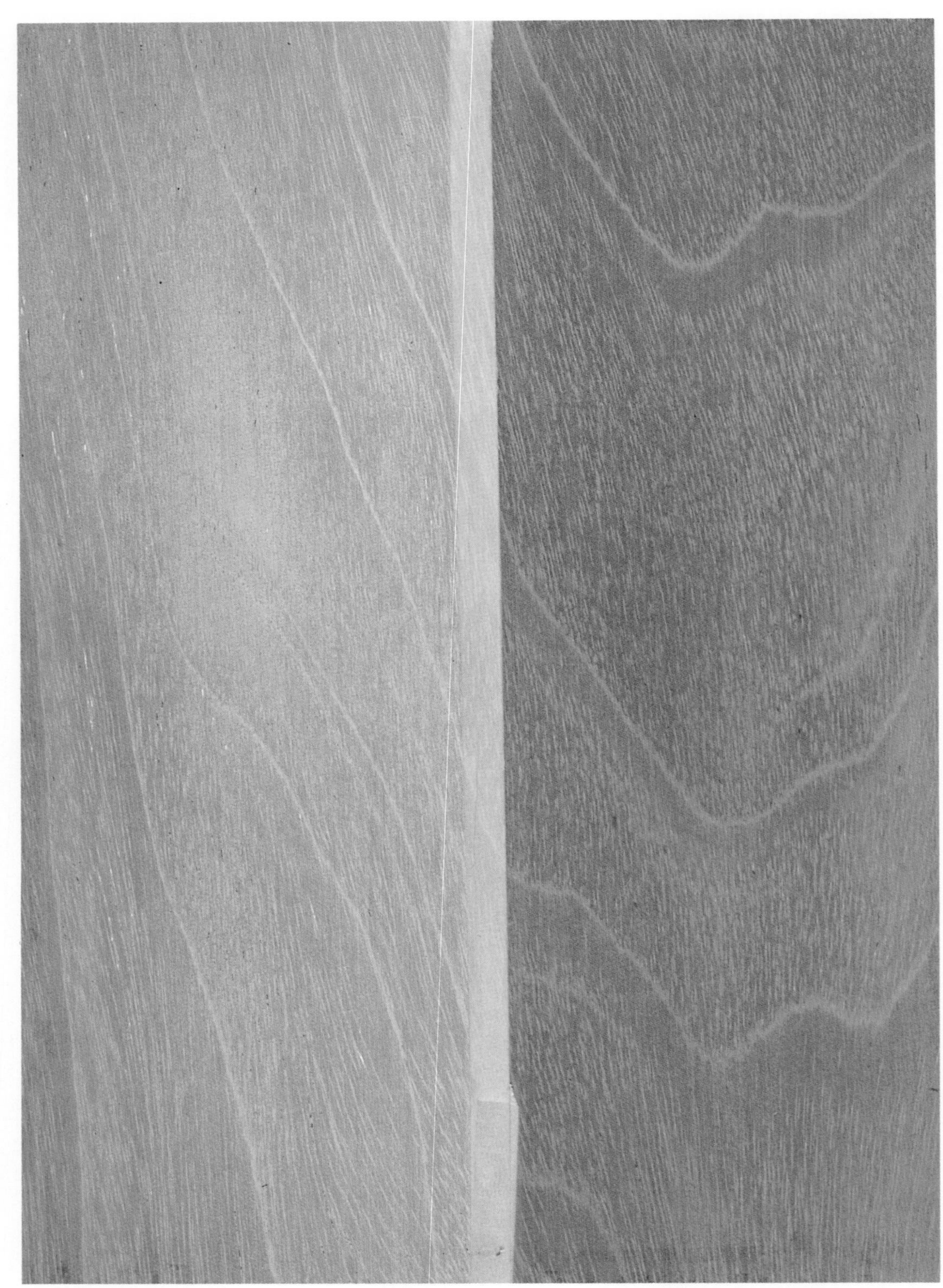

Left: South American mahogany in its natural state. Right: South American mahogany treated with brazilwood extract.

Left: South American mahogany finished with sprayed-on clear lacquer. Right: South American mahogany treated with dichromate.

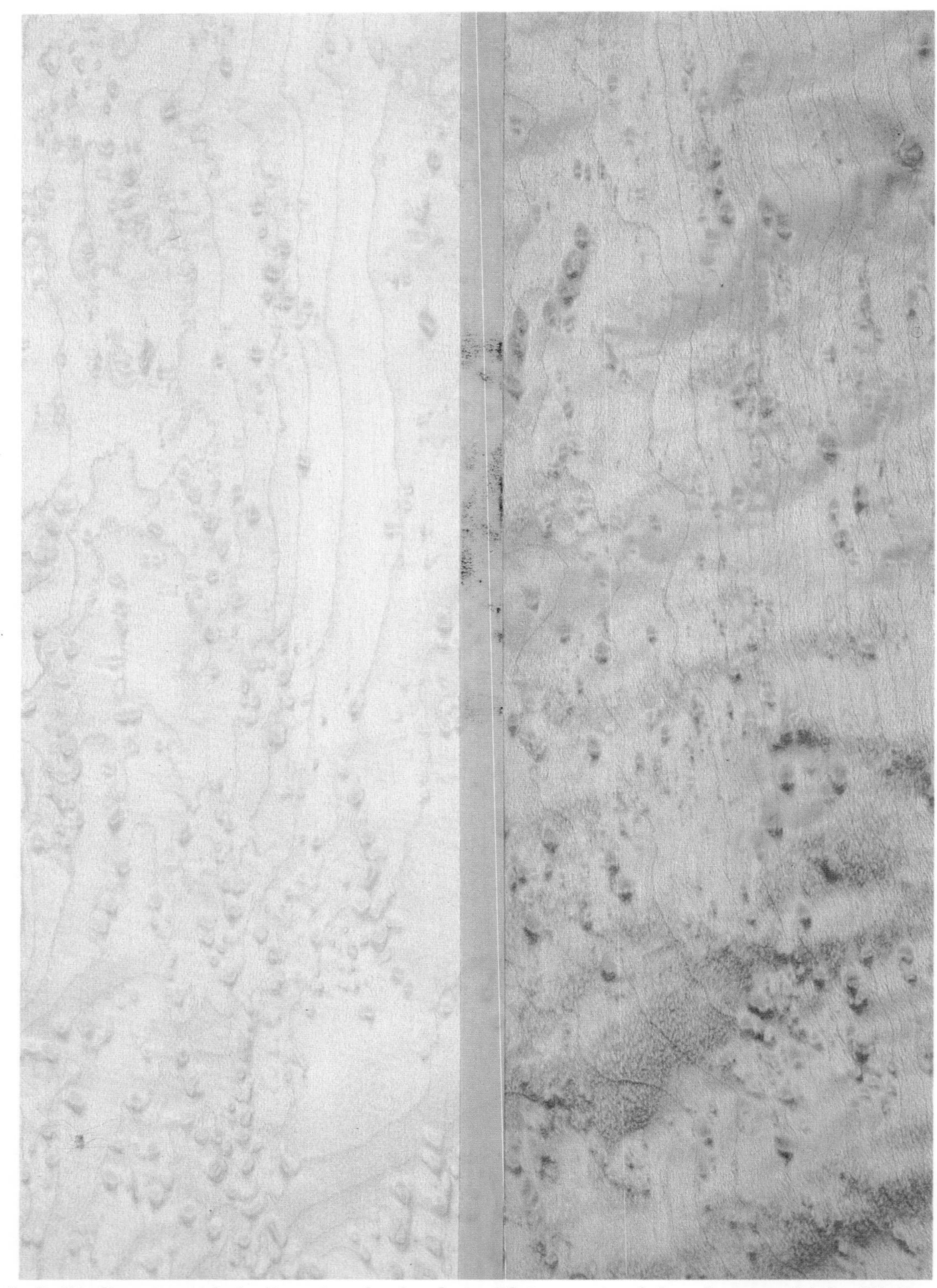

Left: Bird's-eye maple in its natural color, but with two coats of clear lacquer. Right: Bird's-eye maple colored with solution of ferrous sulphate, and coated with two coats of clear lacquer.

Honduras mahagony treated with logwood, dichromate, and lacquer.

Above: Logwood and alum. Below: Brazilwood and alum.

Above: Catechu and potassium dichromate. Below: Brazilwood and potassium dichromate.

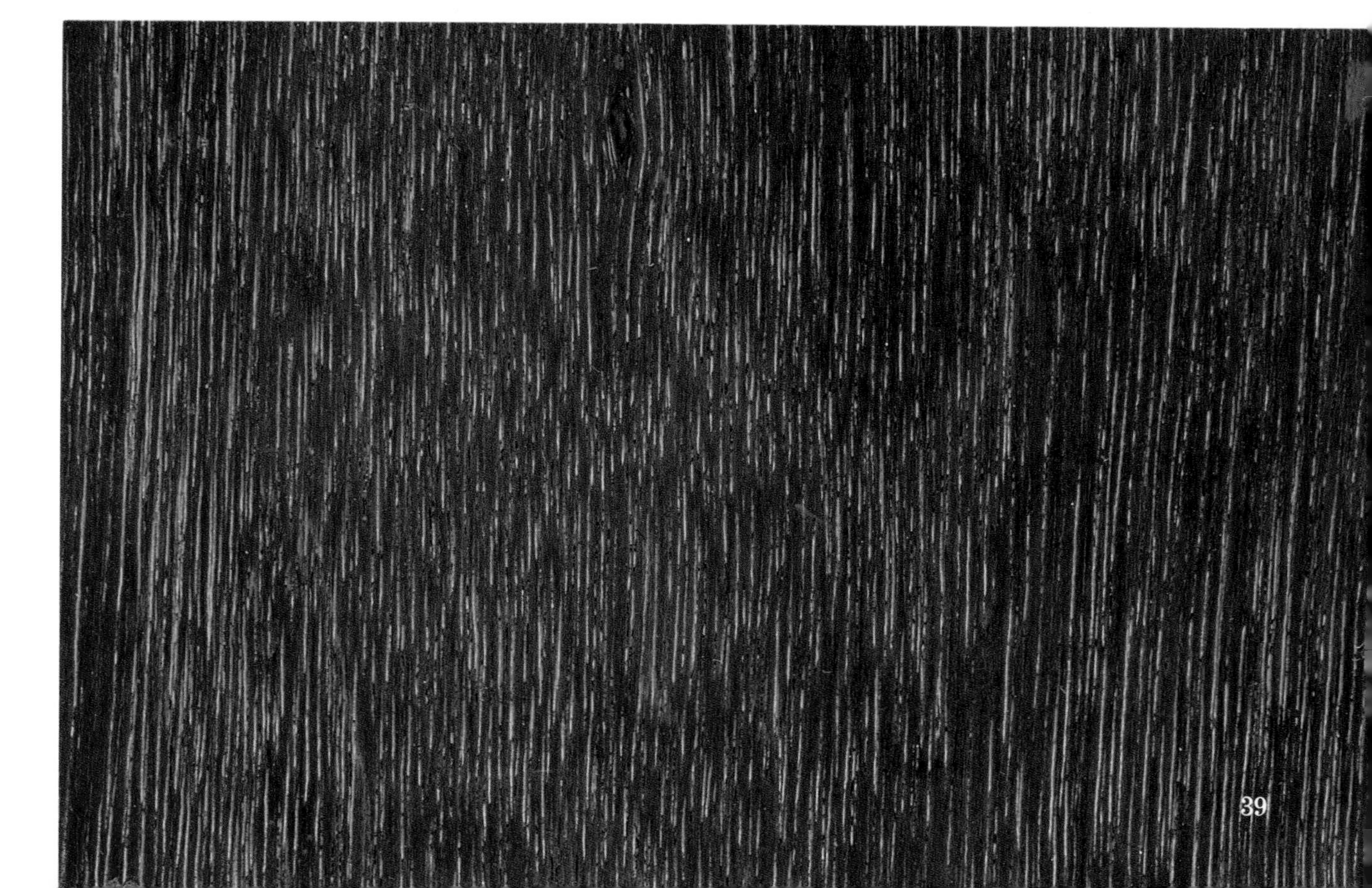

Above: Logwood and copper sulfate. Below: Yellowwood and copper sulfate.

Above: Brazilwood and stannous chloride. Below: Logwood and stannous chloride.

We can change and eventually improve the natural color of the wood through chemical treatment. The sample shown here and the ones shown on pages 43 through 51 have been colored in such a way. See pages 26–30 for a further discussion of chemical treatment of wood. Left: Cherry in its natural state. Right: Cherry washed with lye and rinsed. No finish was applied on either one.

Left: Cherry sponged with potassium dichromate and left unfinished. Right: Cherry sponged with potassium dichromate, and finished with shelliq and clear lacquer.

Left: Cherry in its natural state. Right: Cherry sponged with dichromate. There is no finish on either one.

Left: Cherry sponged with freshly slacked lime and coated with white shelliq. Right: Cherry sponged with freshly slacked lime and finished with garnet shelliq.

Left: Oak in its natural state. Right: Oak washed with lye and rinsed. There is no finish.

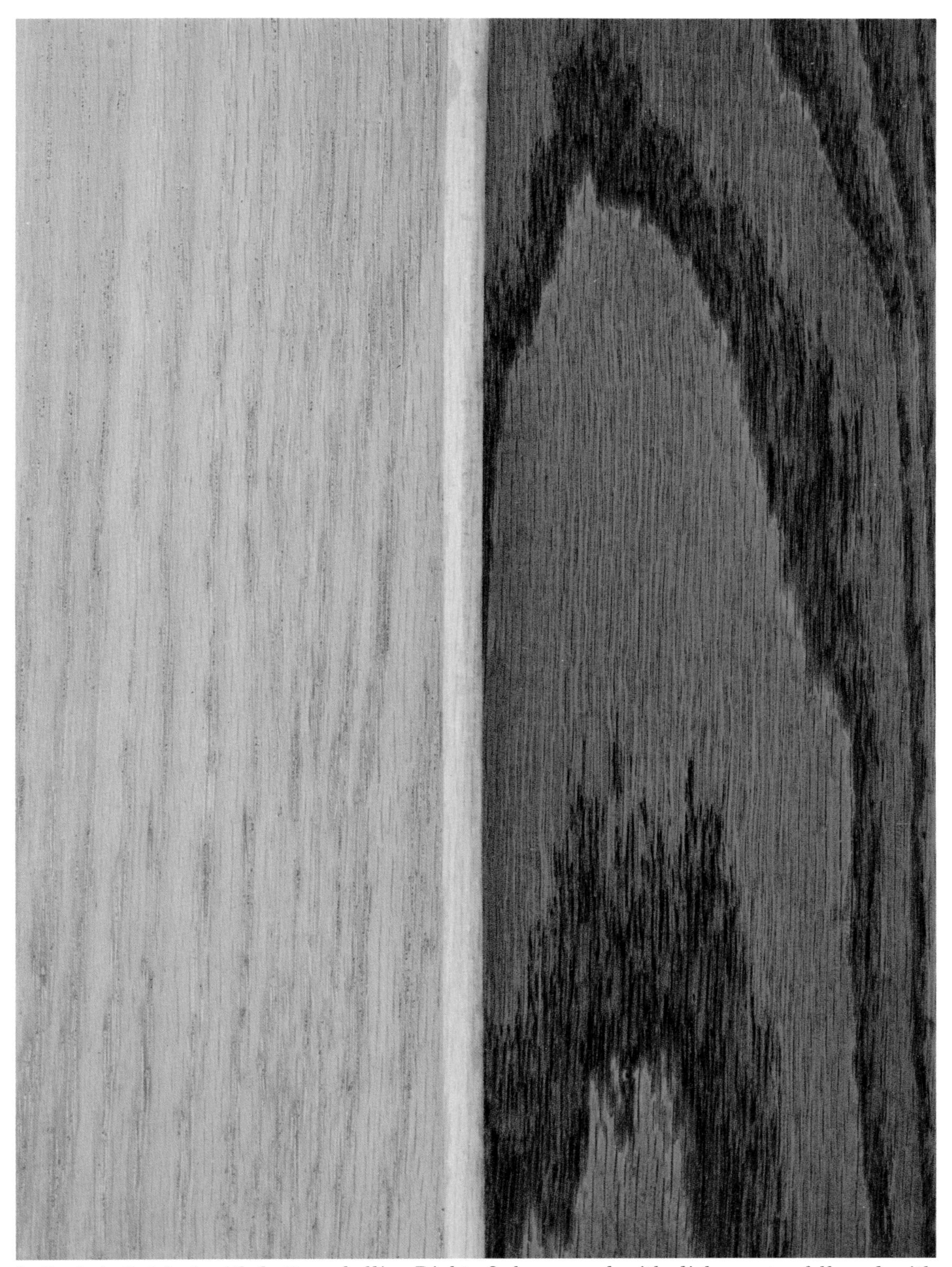

Left: Oak finished with button shelliq. Right: Oak sponged with dichromate, followed with logwood extract.

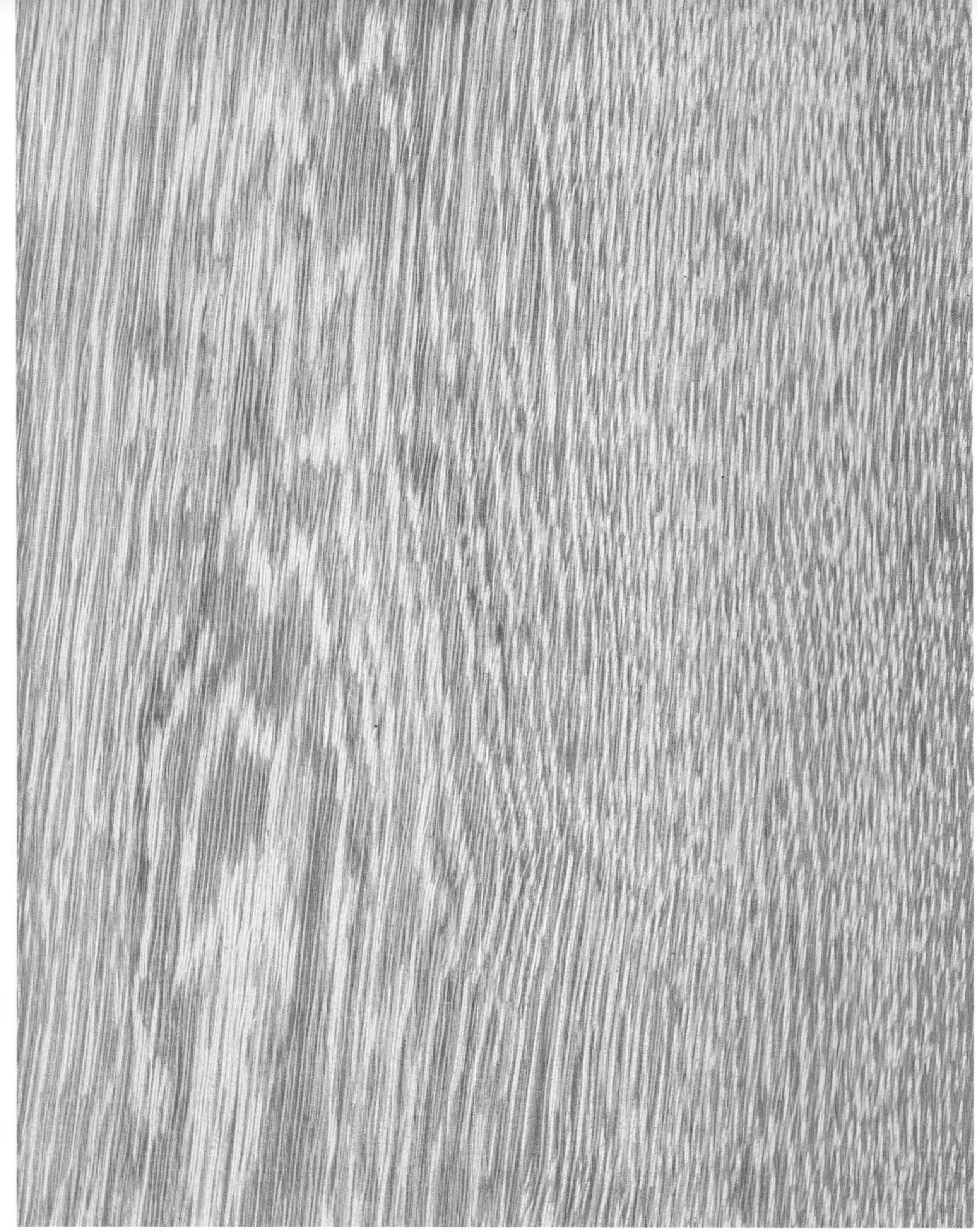

The two oak samples shown here and on the following page are a modern version of the décapé *(washed-off) finish. Both were washed off with a strong solution of warm lye, rinsed, coated with freshly slacked lime, brushed, and finished with two coats of wax emulsion.*

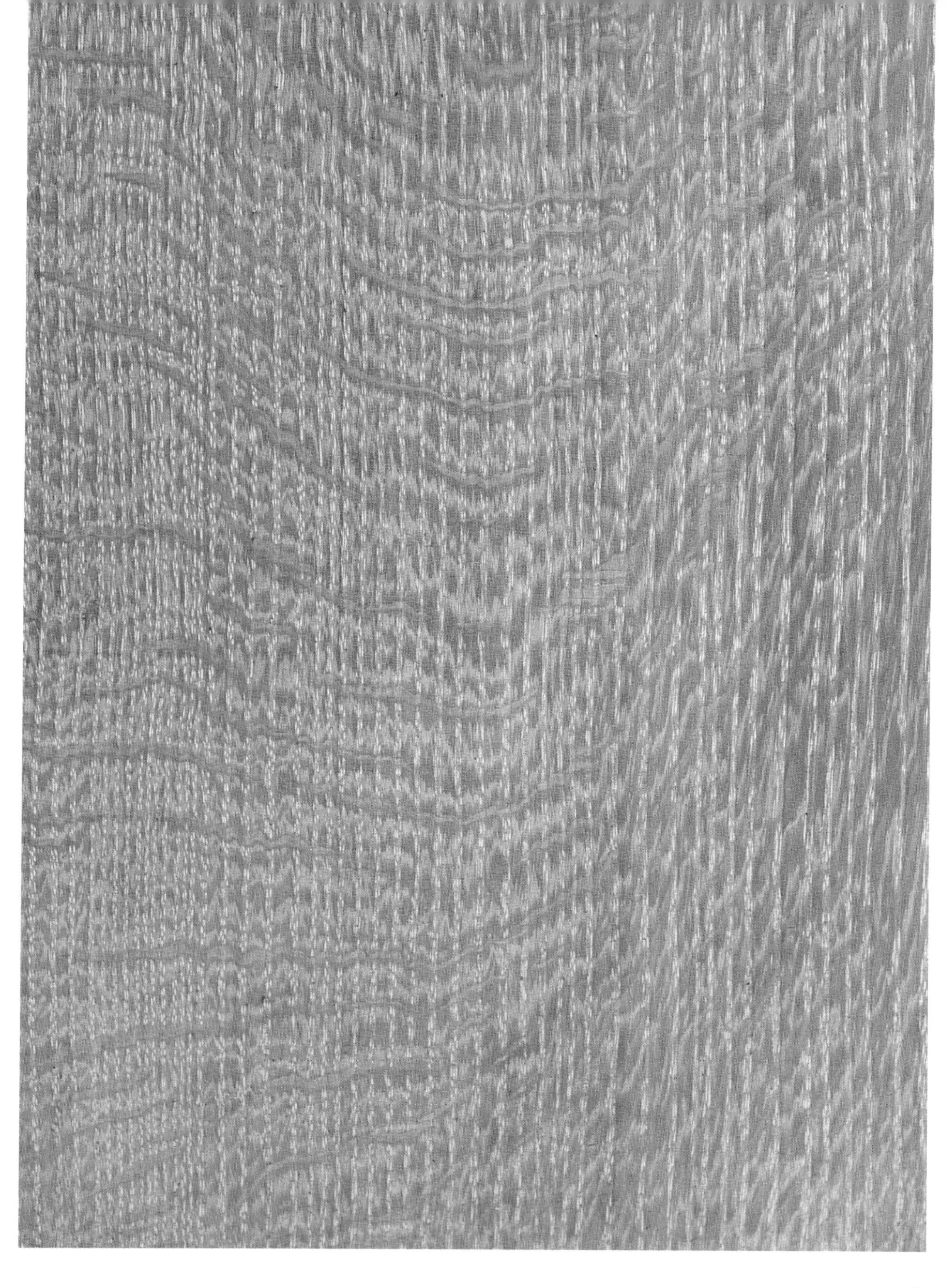

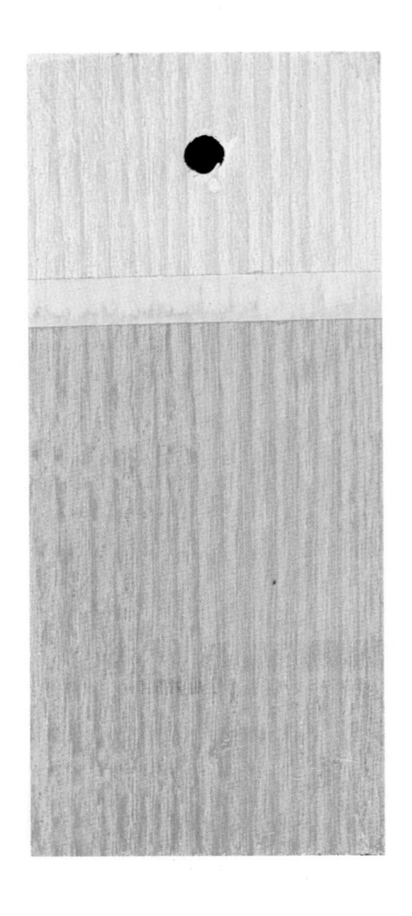

These two ash samples were treated with ammonia gas that did not affect the upper portions (with the hole). Prior to fuming, the lower section of the sample on the left was treated with a solution of tannic acid. The lower section of the sample on the right was treated with logwood extract.

The upper sections of these oak samples were affected by the ammonia gas treatments, but the left corner of the sample on the right was not, because the sap portion of the oak tree contains no tannic acid. The lower section of this sample was treated with logwood extract that compensated for this shortcoming.

In the fairy tale, the sleeping princess opened her beautiful eyes when kissed by the handsome prince. The true beauty of the maplewood shown above was revealed when it was kissed by a solution of ferrous sulphate, after being washed with lye. Below: Spruce that has been pressure-treated against termites and fungi. The chemical injected into the timber emphasizes its markings, and offers interesting decorative effects, especially when crosscut.

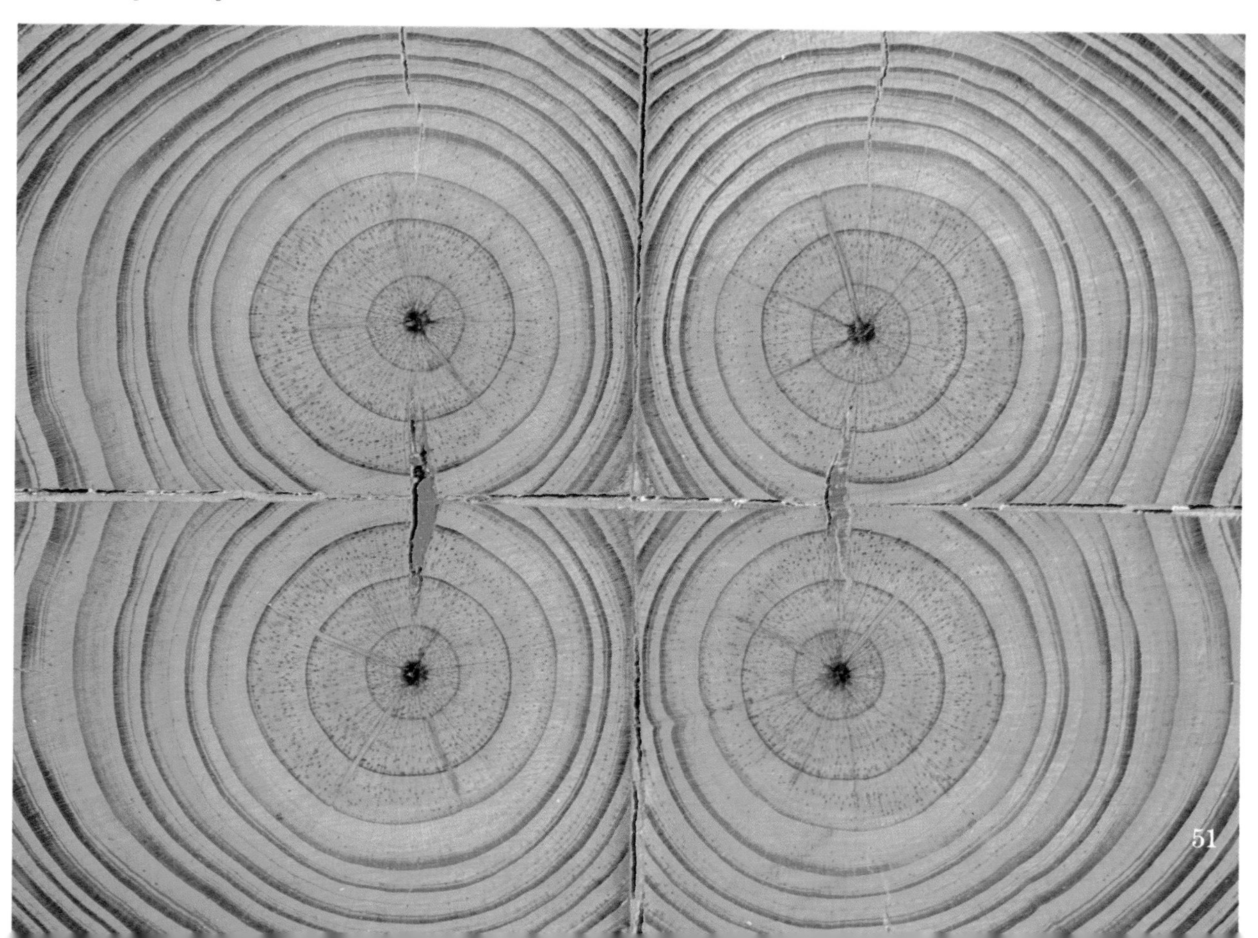

The samples shown on this page and on pages 53 and 54 are French-polished. See pages 96–110 for a discussion of this technique.

In France in the mid-1930s, interior decorators competed against each other to produce an innovation in the trade. Some introduced lumber never used before in cabinetmaking. The two samples shown here were French-polished by me. The French name of the wood shown above is épi de blé *(ear, or spike, of wheat). The one shown below is called* palmier *(palm tree). Both are probably members of the palm-tree family.*

The samples shown on this page and page 56 have been finished via the open-pore French-polishing method discussed on pages 111 and 112. Above: This sample has been dyed with an aniline dye. The piece below has been dyed with a homemade chemical, which consisted of household vinegar in which I soaked scrap-iron junk (see page 23). I baptized this chemical "liquid nightmare." Note the quality of the produced colors.

The samples above and below have been dyed with a combination of logwood extract and dichromate of potassium. Different concentrations were used in each sample, producing thrilling, "live" colors.

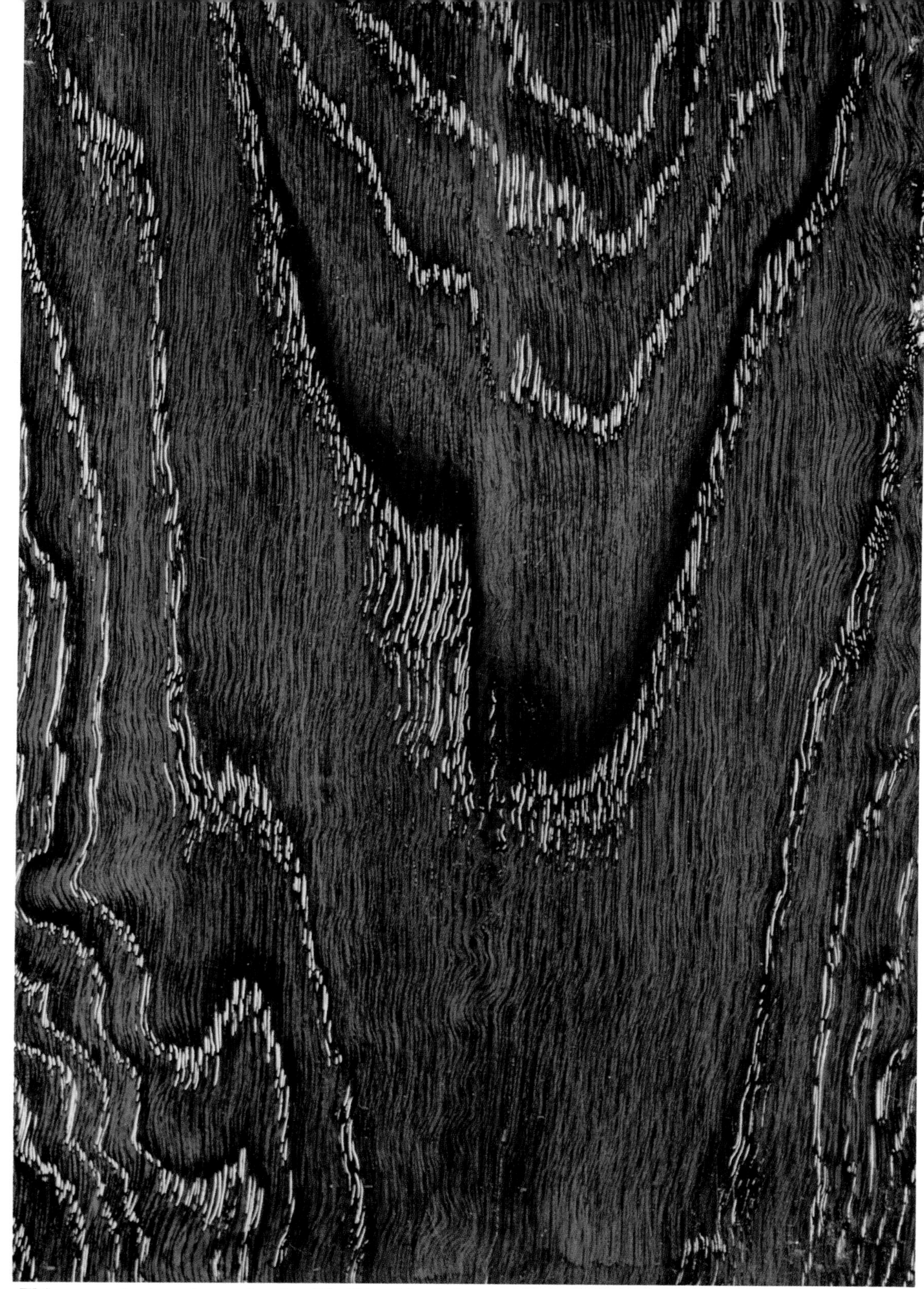

This sample has been dyed with "liquid nightmare", and the pores filled with contrasting colored filler. The samples shown on pages 58–63 have also been decoratively filled. See pages 117–120 for a discussion of the decorative filling of pores.

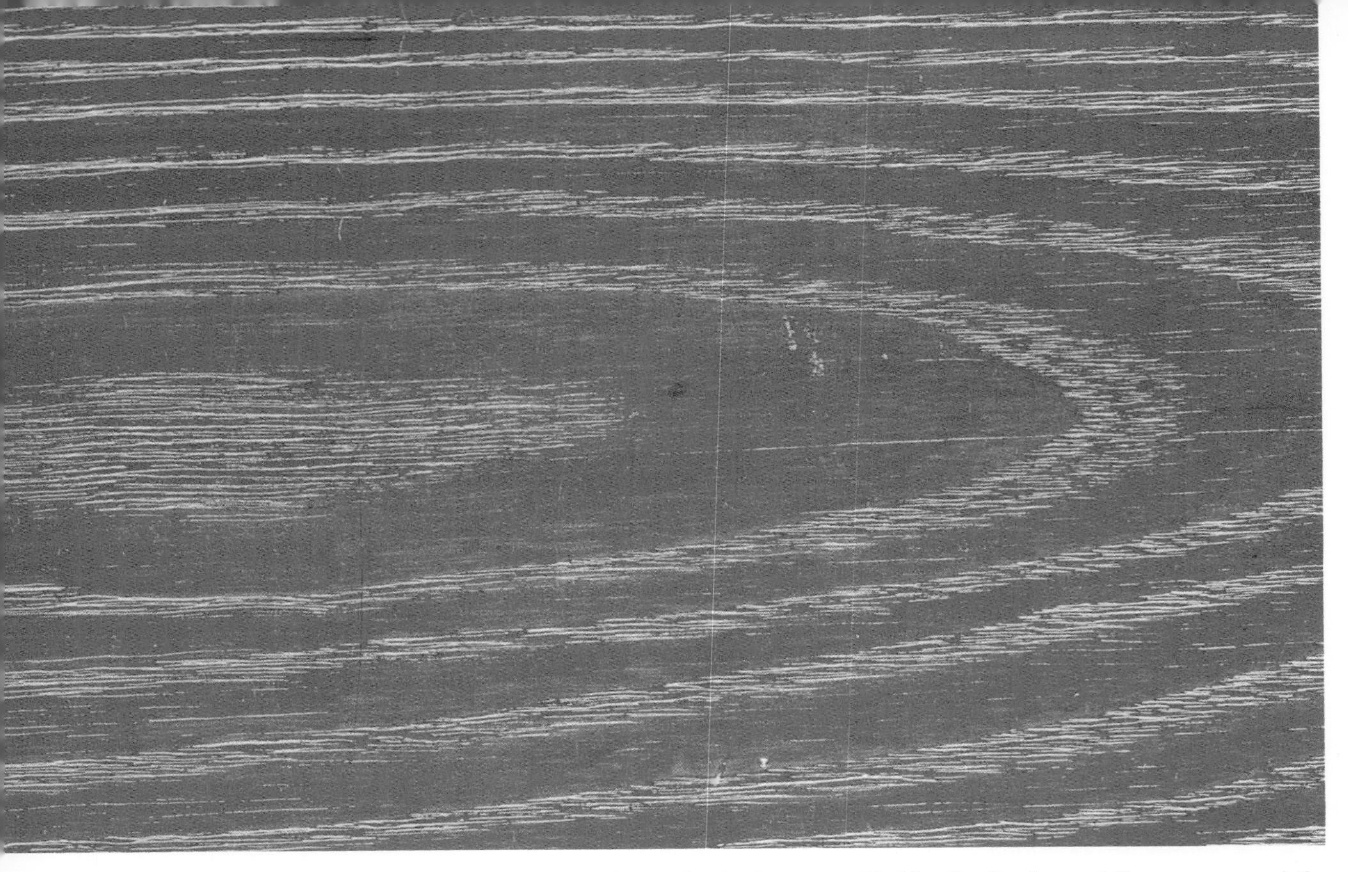

The samples shown here have been dyed with synthetic dyes supplied by the Lockwood Company, and the pores decoratively filled.

The sample above has been dyed with a combination of iron sulfite and alum. The one below has been dyed with a synthetic dye supplied by Arti. Both were decoratively filled.

The sample above was dyed with a synthetic dye from Arti. The sample below was dyed with a combination of logwood and dichromate. Both were decoratively filled.

The sample above was dyed with a combination of brazilwood and dichromate. The one below was dyed with a combination of light lye and tea. Both were decoratively filled.

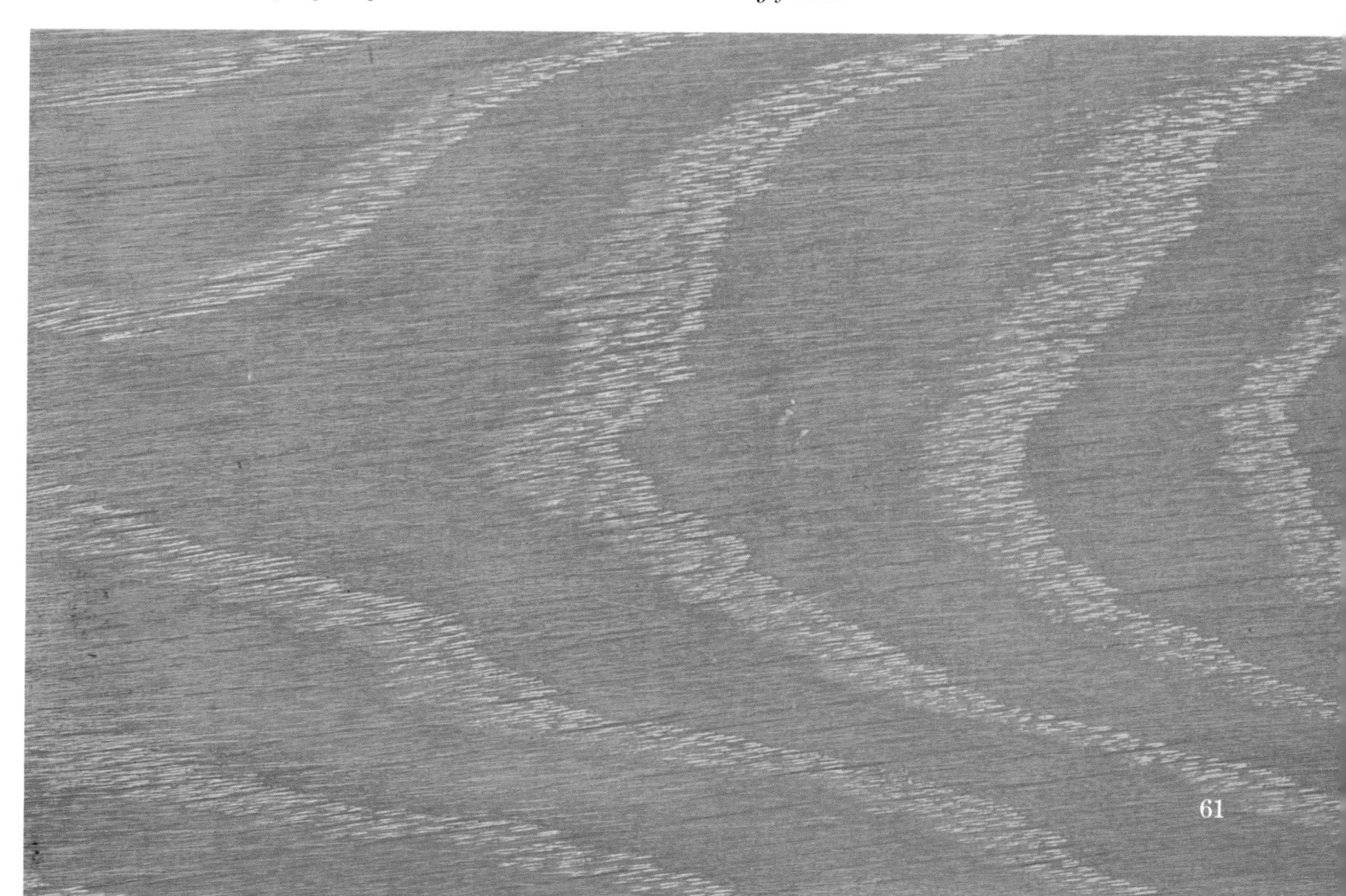

Above: Sample dyed with synthetic dye from Arti. Below: Sample dyed with a combination of tannic acid and dichromate of potassium. Both were decoratively filled.

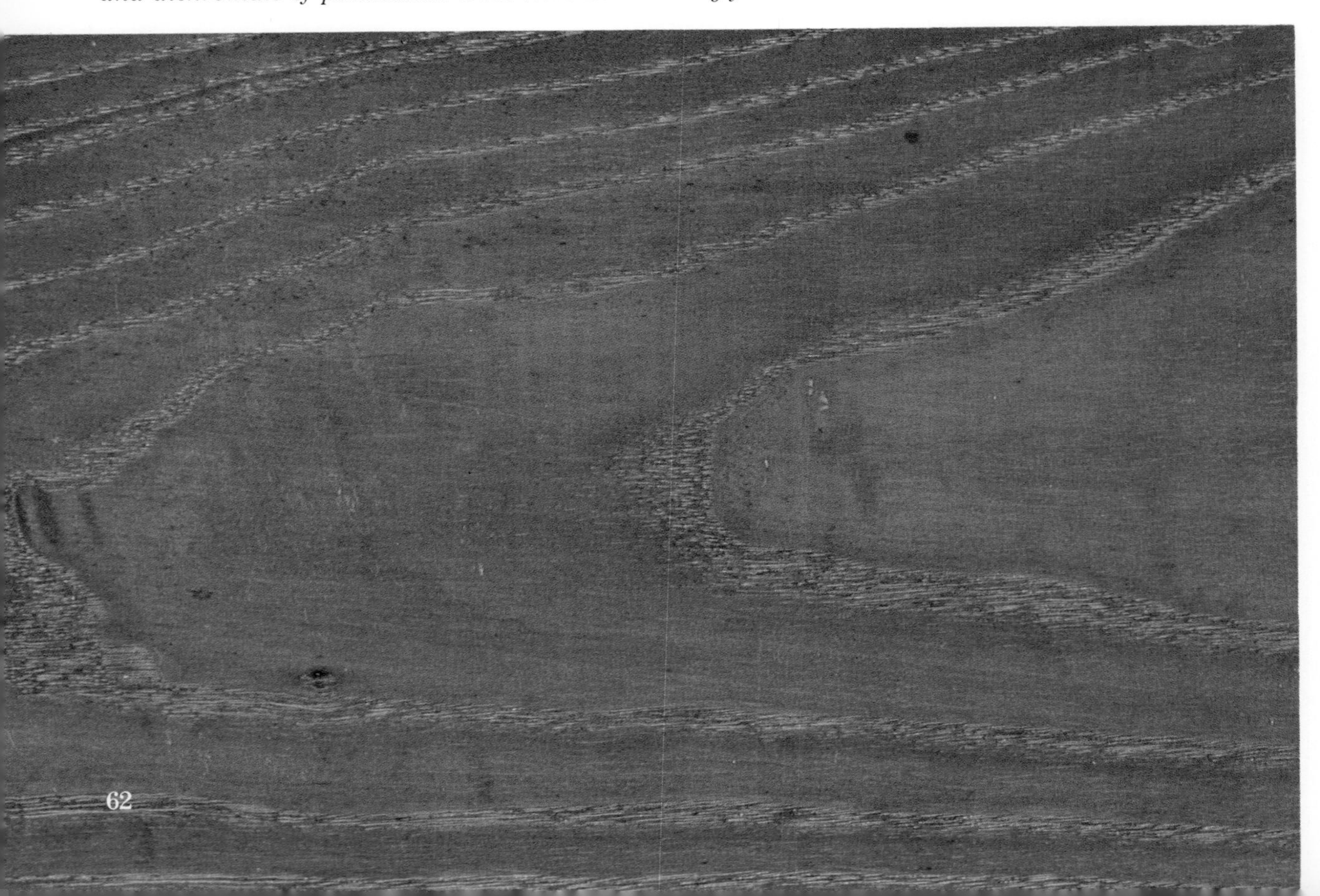

Above: Sample dyed with combination of logwood and alum. Below: Sample dyed with combination of brazilwood and alum. Both were decoratively filled.

The bull shown here and the pieces shown on page 65 all have a scorched finish. See pages 122 and 123 for a description of the scorched finish.

Scorched finishes eventually combined with highlighting and the tinting of the late-wood areas with thin paint.

The samples shown here and on pages 67 through 73 have all been sandblasted. Sandblasting, wire brushing, scorching, or any other technique that emphasizes the three-dimensional character of wood offers limitless opportunities for finishing. See page 124 for a description of the technique of sandblasting.

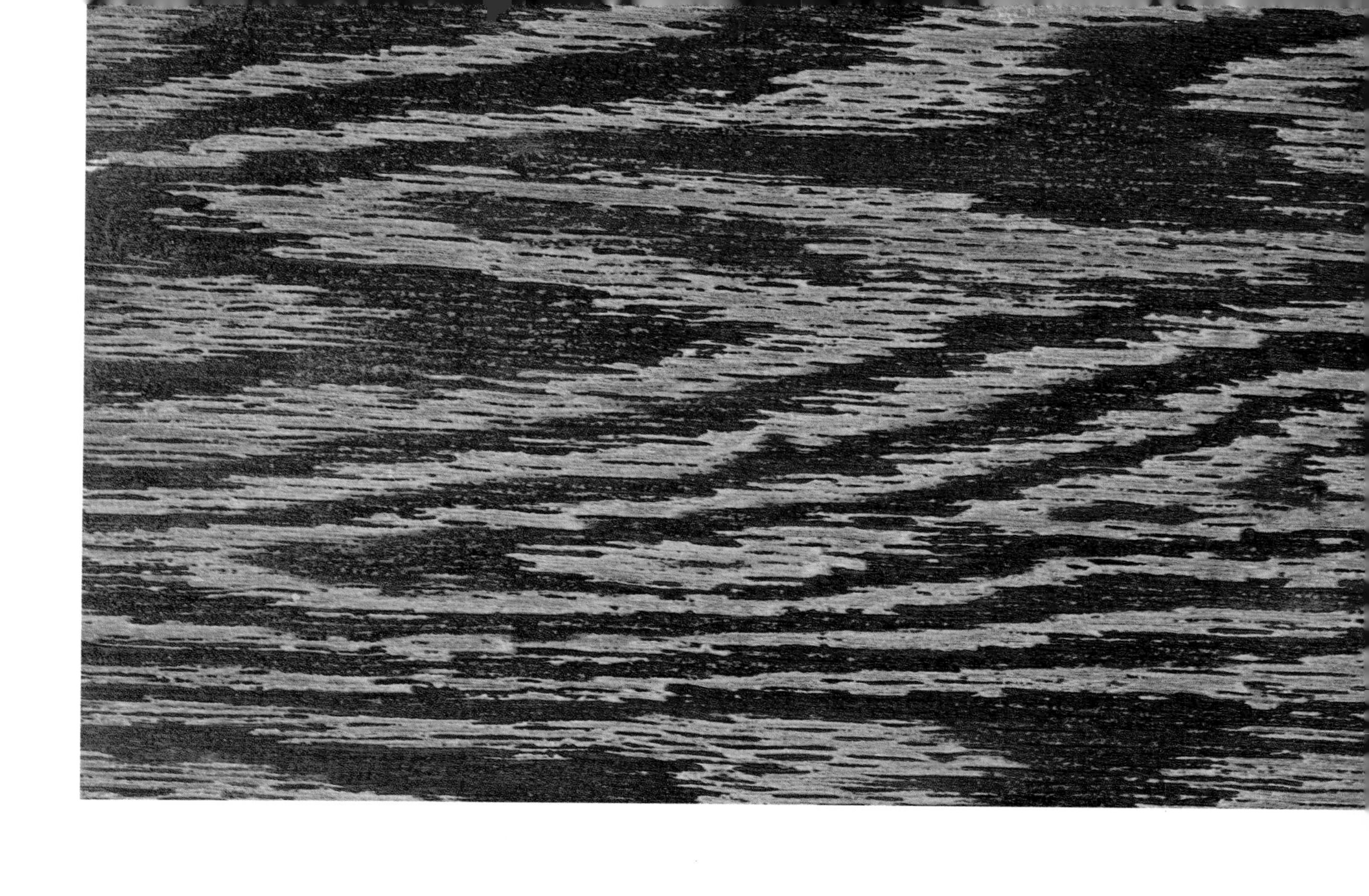

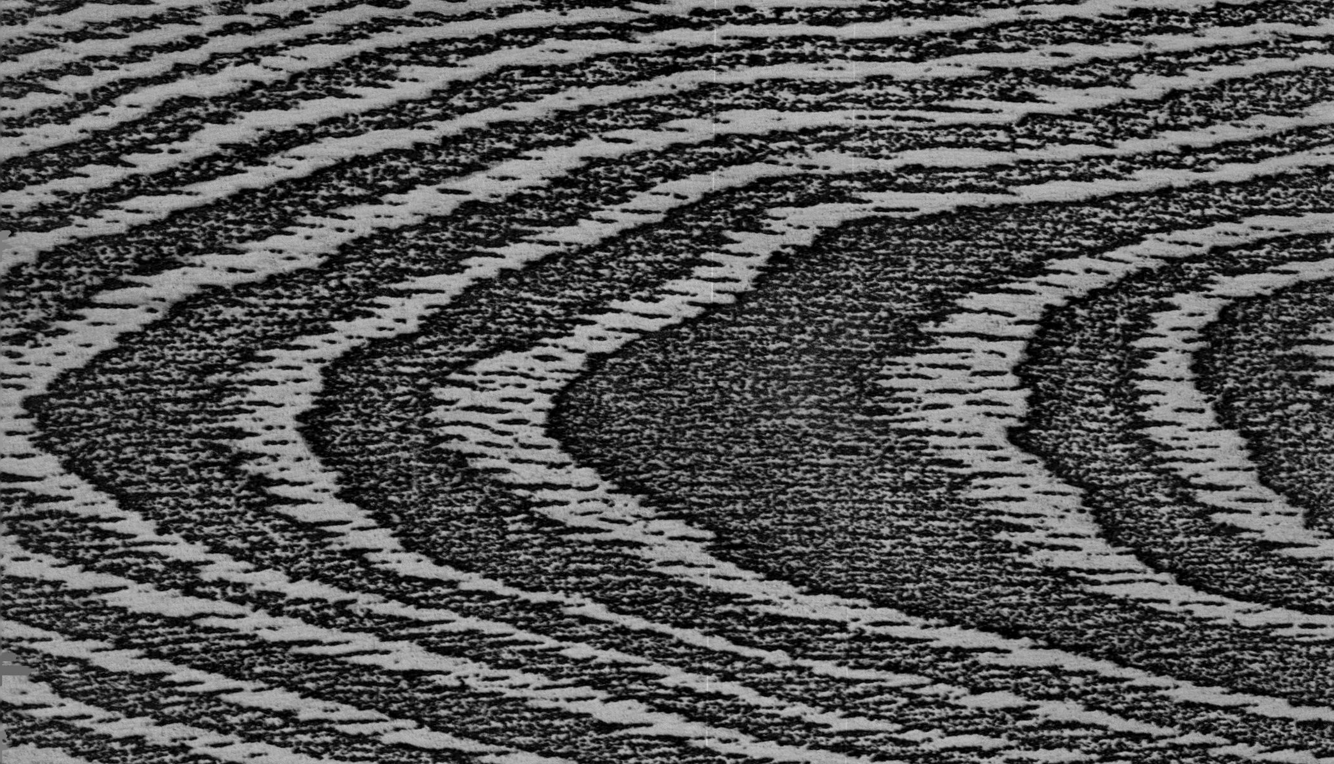

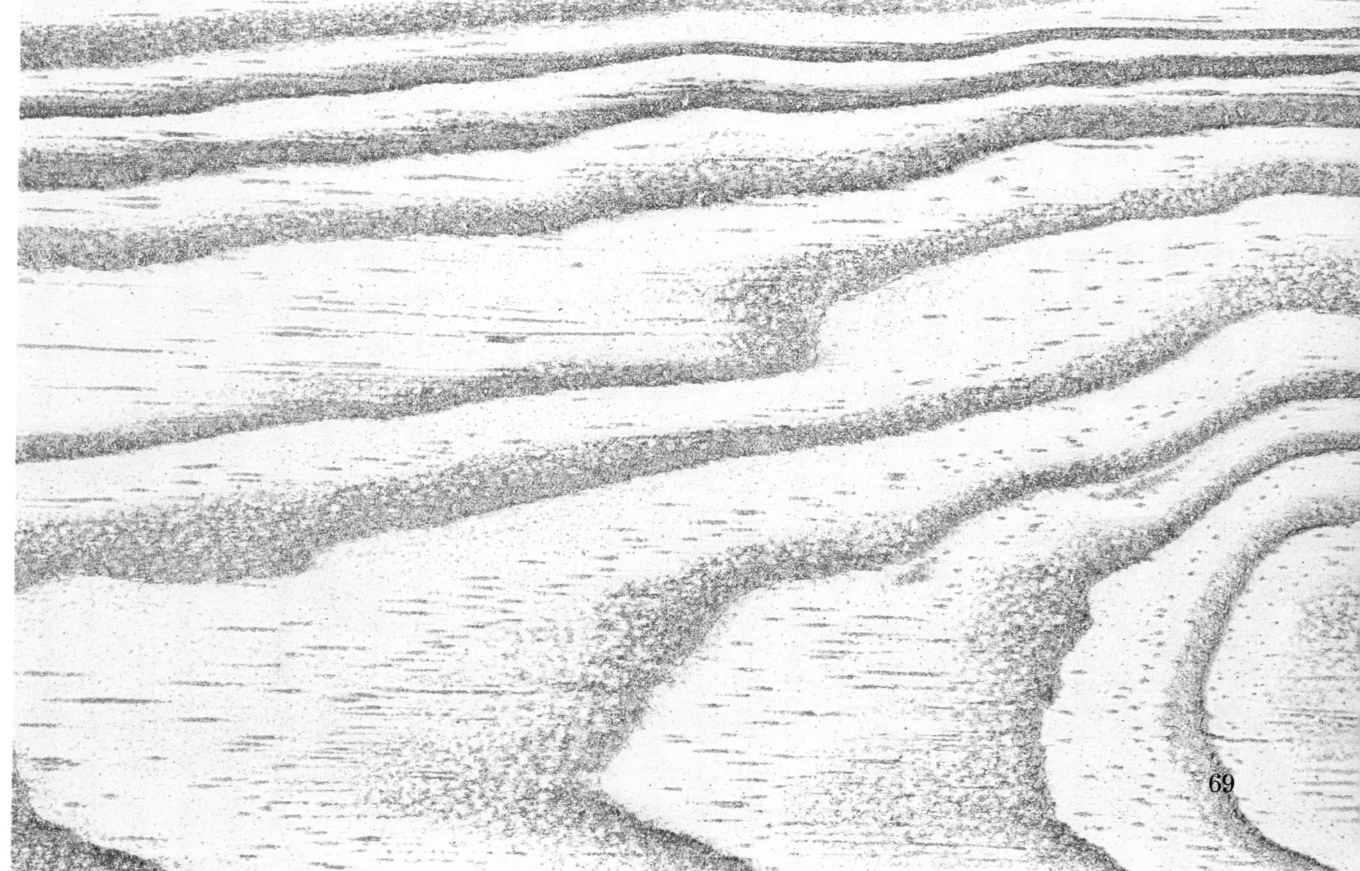

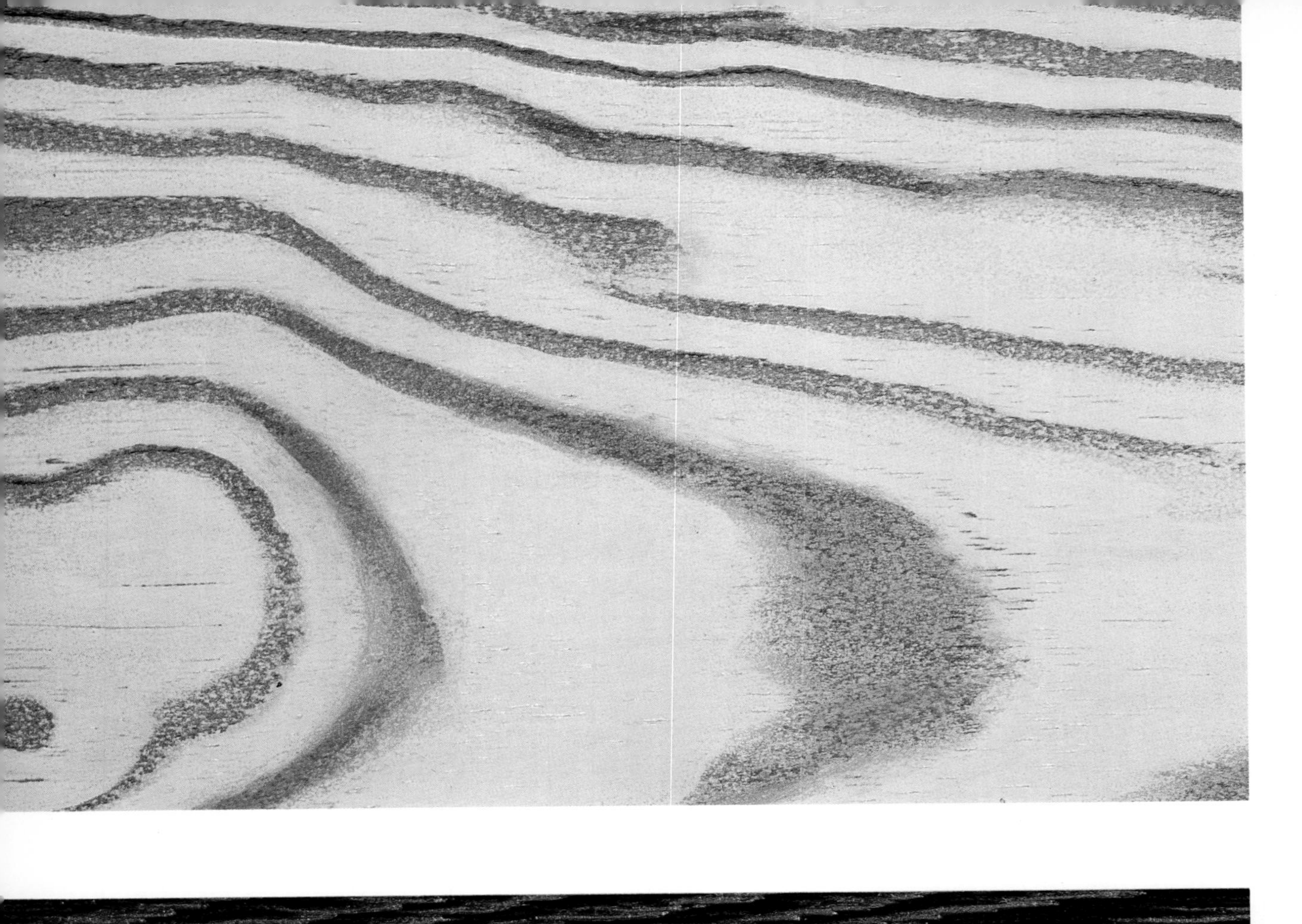

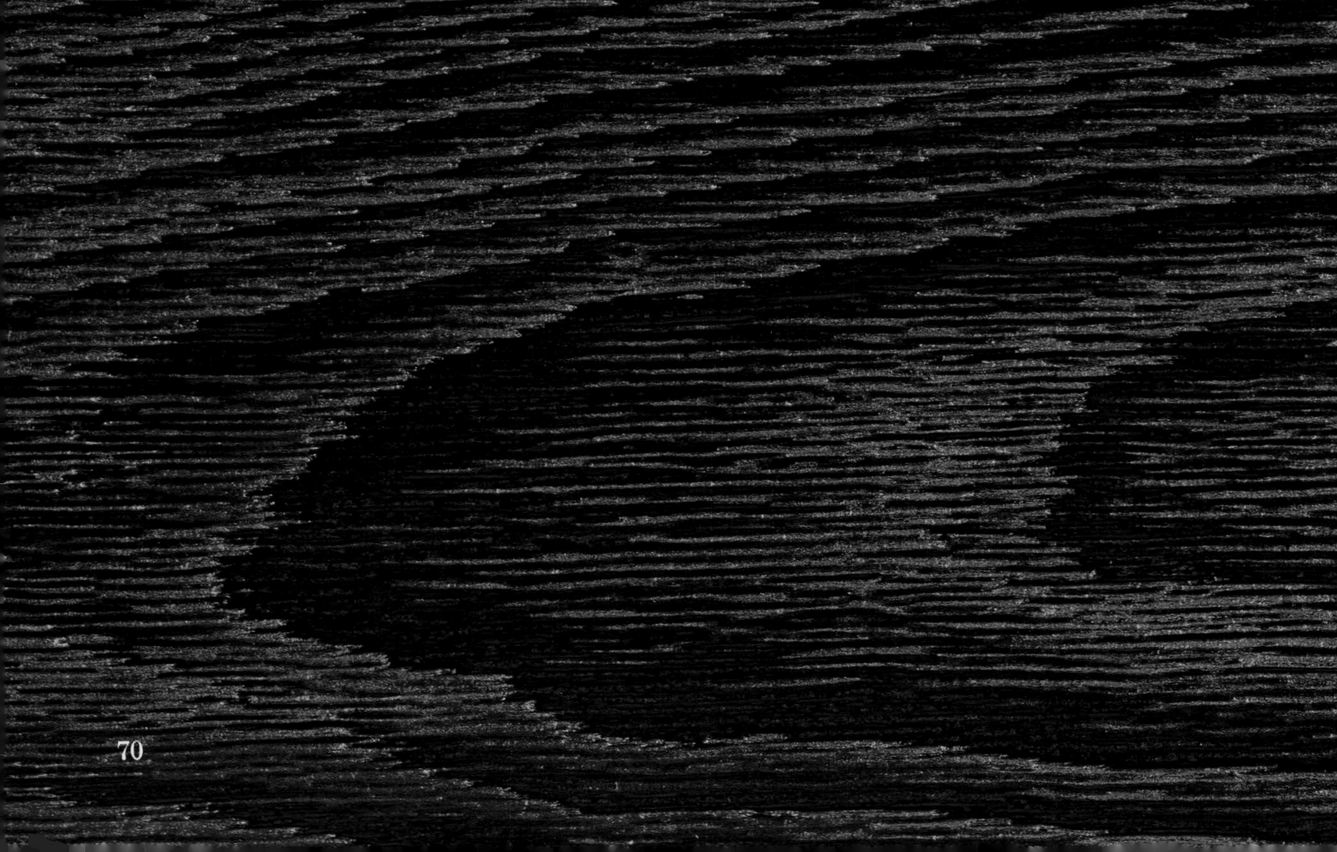

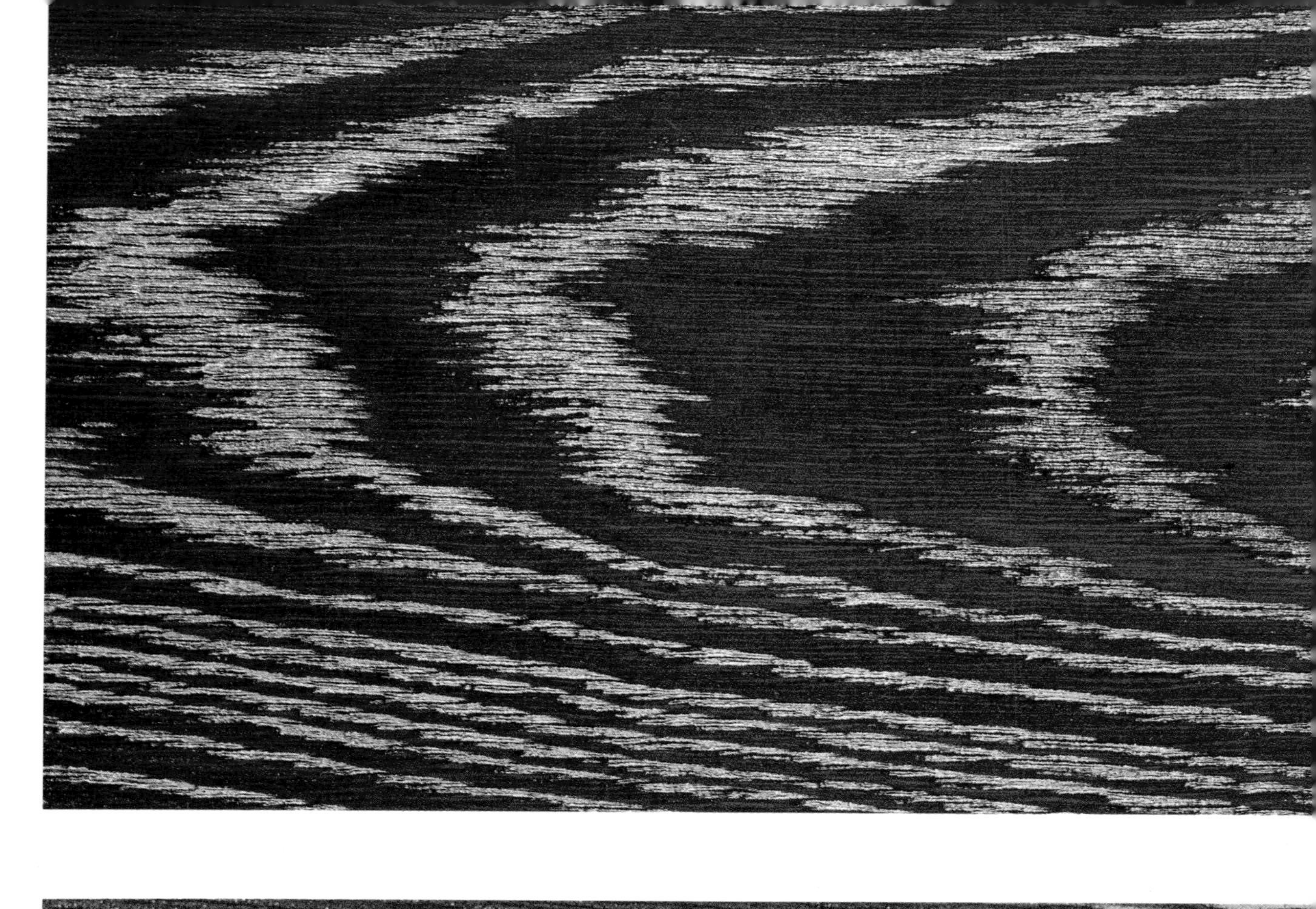

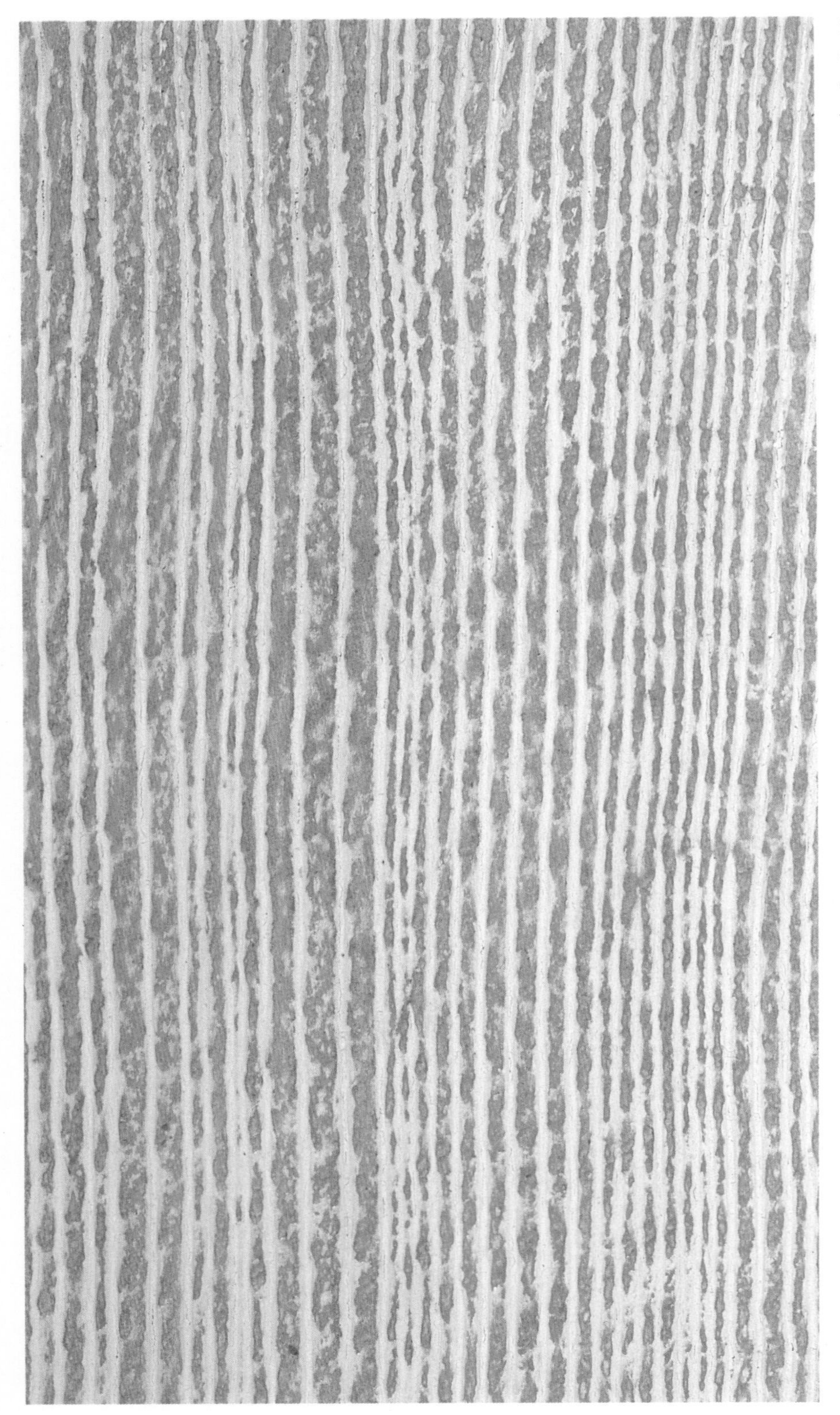

The finish for the white bedroom suite that I describe on pages 126 and 127.

Superimposing shiny and dull areas on sandblasted wood can produce highly decorative effects. This finish is similar to the finish I produced on the bedroom for the Pasha of Marrakech described on pages 124 and 125.

The samples shown on this page and on page 75 were made rough by exposure to weather. Regardless of what causes the roughness, rough wood can take a fine or unusual finish.

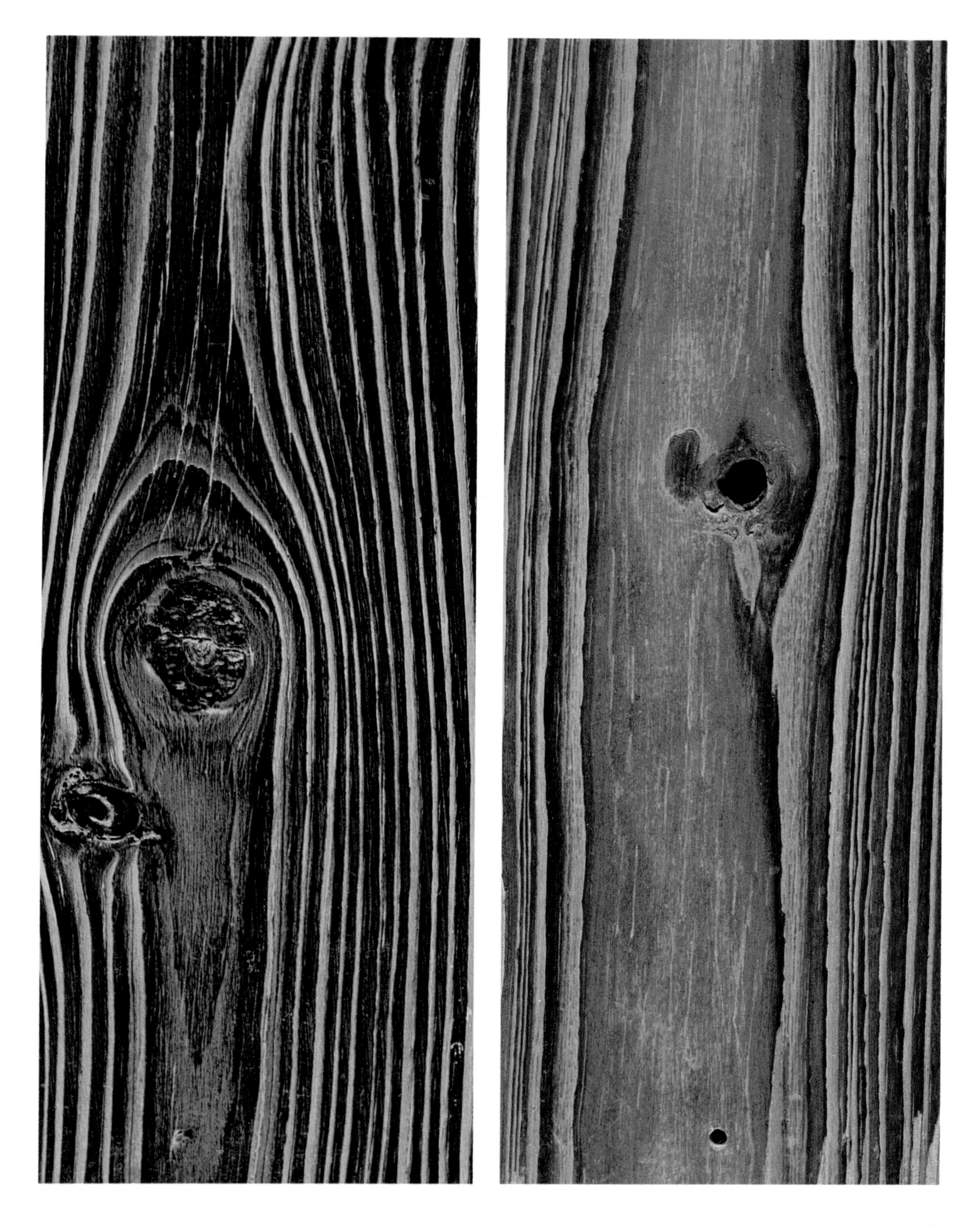

This panel was made rough at the factory probably through wire-brushing. Note how it looks before (above) and after (below) it has been highlighted with dark shelliq.

Above: Highlighting on a commercially roughened board. Below: Highlighting, followed by the coloring of open pores with thin paint.

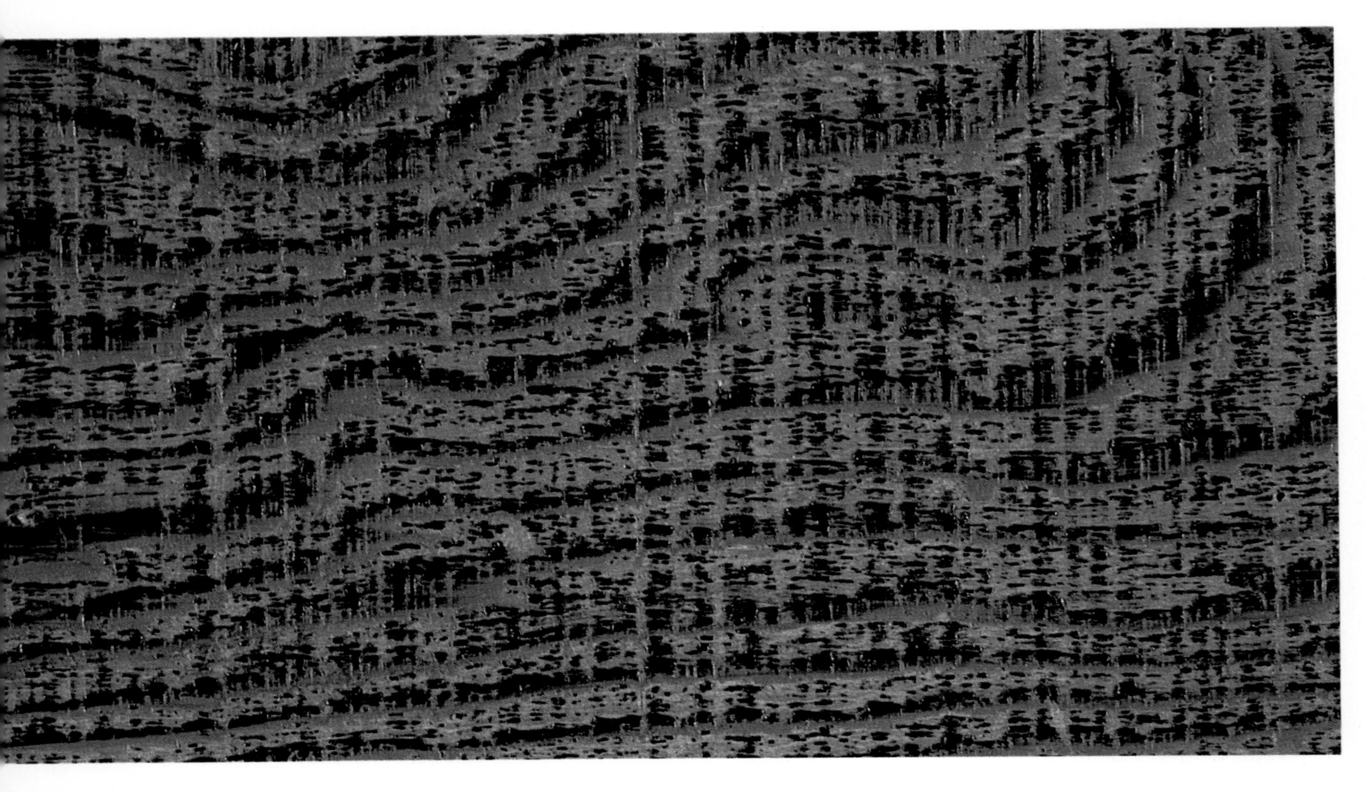

Above and below: Highlighting with decorative pore coloring.

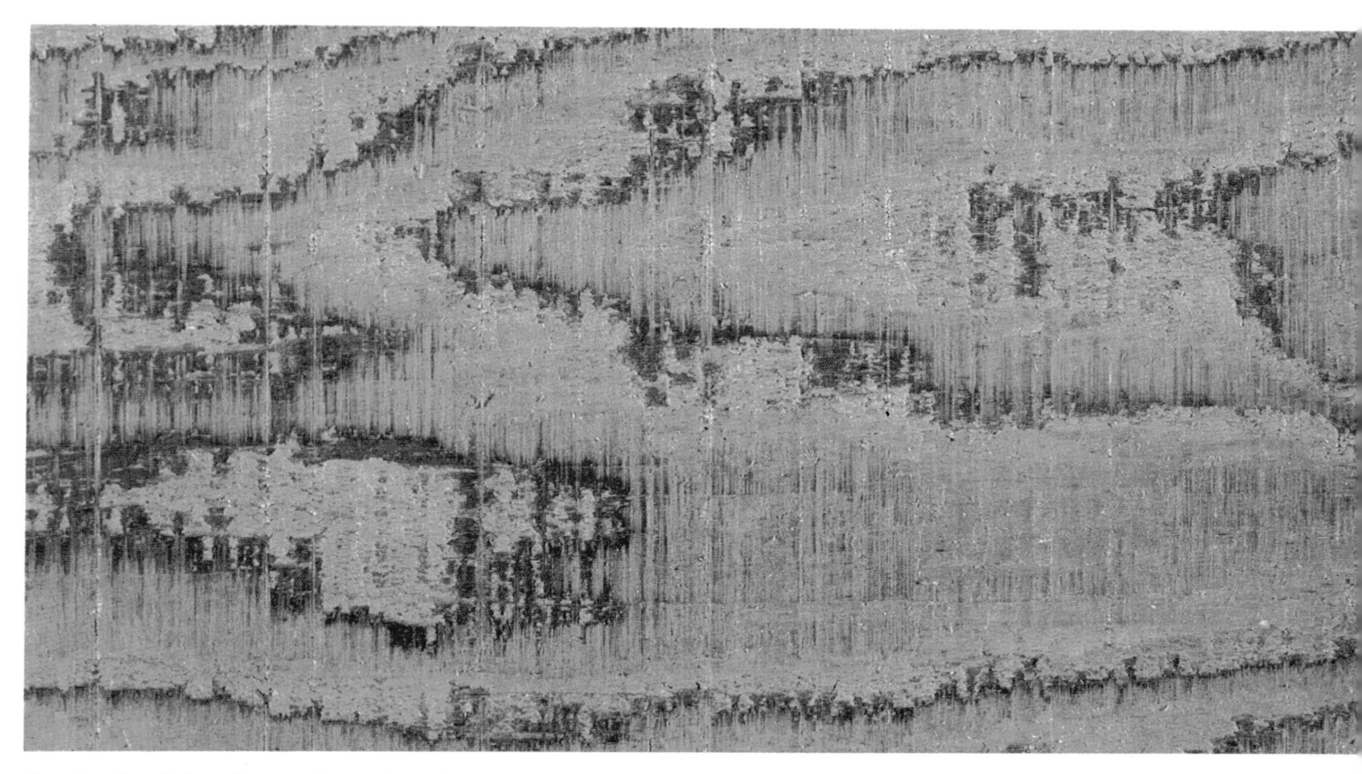

In the local lumberyard, I picked up the factory-made roughened samples shown here and on the following page. An endless variety of finishes can be created on roughened wood.

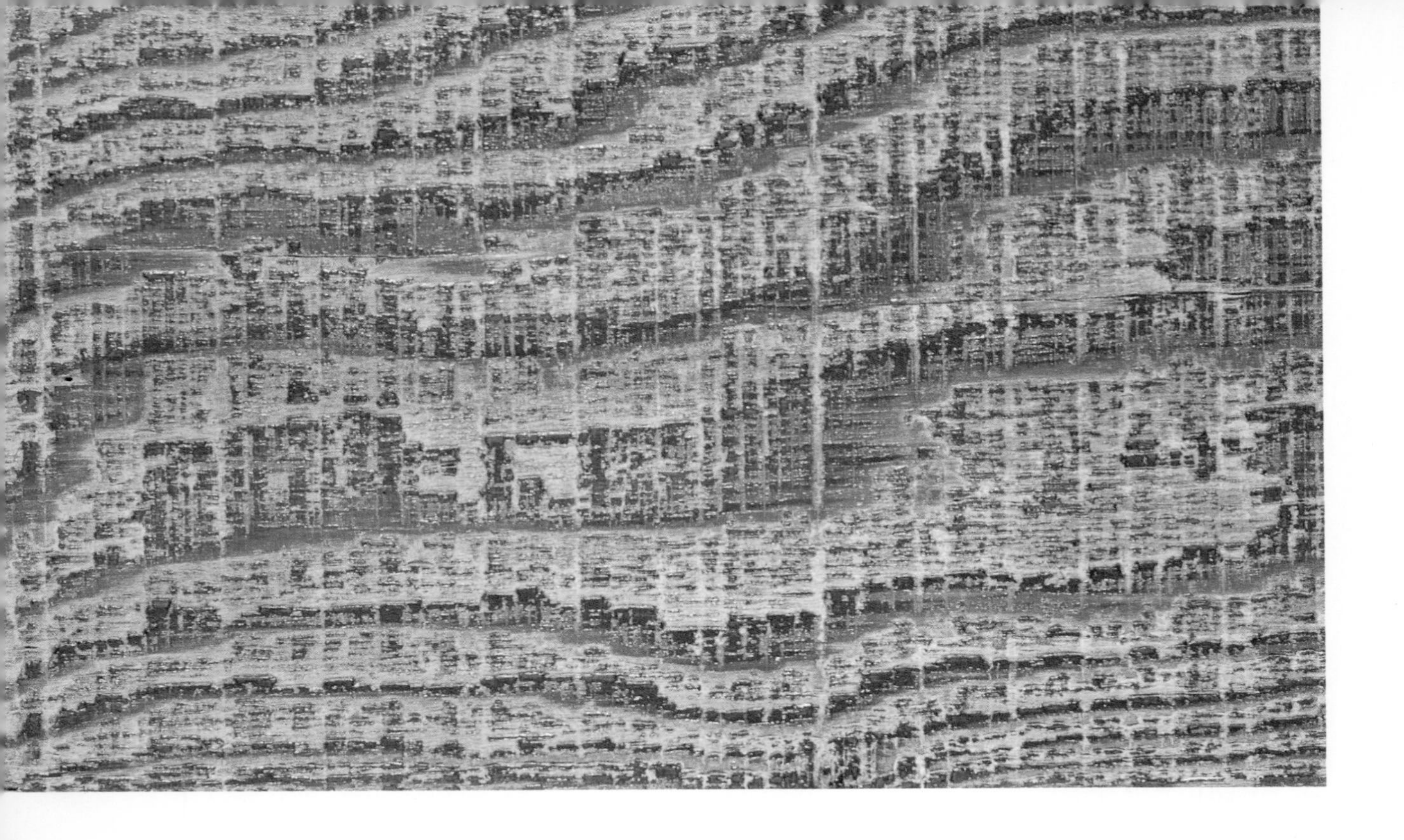

The ideal dye will meet several requirements. First, it will change the color of the wood without covering it. Second, it will penetrate deeply into the wood. Third, the change of color will be permanent; therefore the dye should not be "fugitive." Fourth, the dye will not bleed into the finishing product applied over it. Finally, it will not raise the grain of the wood.

Generally speaking, water-soluble dyes meet all the above requirements except the last one. They do raise the grain. The *ébéniste* had a way to deal with this problem. He wet his wood after the final sanding. The water raised the grain, which he then cut off. The best dyes in the hands of the fine craftsman are without any doubt the water-based ones.

Alcohol-soluble dyes may produce brighter shades, but they have some drawbacks. They fade and they are not easy to work with. In my collection of dyes, only about 10% are alcohol-soluble. I use these mostly for touch-ups or to correct offensive color differences on the finished product.

Alcohol-soluble dyes don't raise the grain of the wood, but because they dry quickly, it is rather difficult to apply them evenly. Therefore, some wood finishers mix these dyes with turpentine. Others add water to slow down this drying; they do not gain much by doing this, and I would question why they use alcohol-soluble dyes at all. I would stick with the proven water dyes.

Modern oil-soluble dyes are excellent in all ways except cost. Dissolved, they are marketed as N.G.R. (non-grain-raising) dyes. They *are* non-grain-raising; moreover, they penetrate deeply into the wood and don't fade. On the production line, they are a blessing. For the fine finisher, water-soluble dyes are best.

"Staining-Dyes"

Consider the following experiment. On pages 18 and 19, we reduced a handful of Colorado earth into fine red pigment. Now, let's mix this red powder with some varnish. We are now ready to thin down this heavy mixture, and for this we will use mineral spirit. So far this experiment is identical to the one discussed on pages 18 and 19. Let's, however, dissolve some oil-soluble red dye in this mineral spirit, instead of the turpentine used in that experiment.

Should this mixture be considered a stain or a dye? It contains the classic composition of a stain, such as a pigment, binder, and carrier. The pigment is the red Colorado dust, the binder the varnish, but the carrier, the mineral spirit, is also a dye. This solution is actually a stain-dye combination.

I stated earlier that fine wood finishers don't use stains, because stains are always covering up, to some extent, the natural markings of the wood. We work instead with dyes, which change the color of the wood without concealing its markings. This general rule is sometimes broken with the use of the "stain-dye" combinations sold under various trade names.

Let's examine some facts about the fine dust that was used in the example of a stain-dye just given. A single cubic inch is approximately 18 cubic centimetres (a cubic centimetre is a theoretical measuring unit that is one centimetre long, wide, and tall). On a rainy day, the air in a cubic centimetre will contain 32,000 pieces of solid particles that we call dust. The air in your room carries close to two million dust particles per cubic centimetre, and the air close to the ceiling contains over five million per cubic centimetre. The purest air in the United States is that around the top of Mount McKinley; it has only 210 dust particles per cubic centimetre. There is considerable difference between the "fine" dust we produce in the mortar and the fine dust the air carries around the top of Mount McKinley.

Though we cannot produce industrially, as yet, dust as fine as the dust this air carries, we are making progress. Modern technology is producing unpalpable fine dust that makes up super-pigments and super-stains. The use of these superfine pigments combined with richly colored carriers or solvents produces stain-dyes of superior quality.

The formula for these stain-dyes does not differ from the formula for regular stains; the ingredients do. The pigment is the unpalpably fine dust of a coloring solid, and the carrier is actually a dye. The third component, the binder, has not been changed.

It would be totally contrary to common sense to ignore these superior stain-dyes, or to advise you against using them. They offer great advantages. The dye contained in them is usually a very potent one, and its solvent not only penetrates, it will not raise the grain of the wood. The pigment is so finely ground it will enter the microscopic openings of the wood instead of forming a film or a colored layer on top. Very little of this finely ground pigment will remain on the stain-dye-colored wood. For those who are looking for uniformity of the colored wood, these stain-dyes are definitely an asset.

As I've mentioned before, the pigment content of these products makes them somewhat like thinned-down paints. However, they have two characteristics the thinned-down paints do not: the amount of pigment remaining on the wood is reduced, and the pigment contributes to the permanency of the new color. These stain-dyes are the best for any wood used outdoors, on items where the cost factor is crucial, and when revealing the maximum beauty of the wood is not the most important factor.

Stains, Dyes, and Finishes

We have just established the fact that stains and dyes can be mixed. Most of the commercial "stains" on the market are actually a combination of the two. These stain-dyes are unbeatable for outdoor use, since they are far less "fugitive" than even the best dyes alone would be.

Now, let's go one step further and examine what happens when we try to combine stains, dyes, and finishes. One of the oldest finishes used in the trade is beeswax. Let's experiment with this wax.

Take some oil-soluble dark walnut dye and dissolve it in either mineral spirit or in plain gasoline. This mixture—a dark-brown liquid—is now the solvent.

In a double boiler, melt some plain beeswax away from any fire hazard. When the wax is melted, thin it with the dark-brown solvent, and let it cool down. When the wax has cooled, the result will be a pleasant brown paste wax.

If you use this wax on a piece of well-sandpapered pine board, applying the wax generously and wiping up the excess, not only will you coat the board with a protective coating, you will also change its color. It will acquire the color of the dye used in the solvent. In a single operation, you have dyed and waxed a pine board and demonstrated the fact that dyes or stains can be combined with finishes.

All finishes can be combined with dyes or stains. Evidently, if you want to combine shellac with a dye, the dye must be the alcohol-soluble type. With varnishes, lacquers and oil finishes, oil-soluble dye has to be used.

About twenty years ago, tung oil was not well known among wood finishers. This excellent, yet simple, finishing product has grown in importance; today, it sells well. Tung oil is produced in Georgia, Alabama, and Mississippi, and processed there. It is the main ingredient of the so-called Danish finishes. Tung oil helps the inexperienced finisher produce a decent finish with little effort.

Tung oil and the Danish finishes can and are frequently combined with dyes and pigments. These types of finishes, a combination of finishing oils, oil-soluble dyes, and unpalpable pigments, are already on the market in the United States. The best known among them are the Minwax® and the Watco® products. They are attractively presented and easy to use, though costly. You and I can actually make such finishes out of simple ingredients in our own shops, but it is a question of whether the savings are worth the effort.

Making Wood Smoother or Rougher

Wood's natural beauty can also be improved by changing its tactile quality, that is, by making it smoother or rougher. The smoother the wood is made, the more the hidden beauty of its grain is revealed; this is the ultimate goal. In this chapter I will discuss the tools used to make the wood smoother. In the following two chapters, I will discuss the products and methods involved.

Tools and Abrasives

Tools and/or abrasives are used to make the wood smoother. The tools needed are usually used by woodworkers, not wood finishers. However, wood finishers should keep a couple of block planes, three or four chisels, and a few flat scrapers handy in their toolboxes. These tools should be kept clean and well sharpened.

Wood finishers should learn how to use these tools properly, maintain them, and keep them sharp. Presently in the United States there is only one school where *fine* wood finishing is being taught, but there are many schools where woodworking can be learned and where the wood finisher can learn to use and maintain the tools. Wood finishers can also learn how to use and maintain these tools properly through excellent articles that appear in trade newspapers.

The flat scraper is one tool that is frequently misused. Used improperly, it only succeeds in scraping the wood. Properly sharpened and used in the correct manner, it produces shavings like those produced by some fine block planes, and cleans and smooths wood as well as sandpaper.

An article on the flat scraper appears in the May 1986 issue of *Fine Woodworking*. Written by Stephen Proctor, it explains clearly and concisely what a flat scraper is, what it can do, how to care for it, and how to use it. I recommend it to every wood finisher who is interested in learning about this tool. For those of you who can't find this article, the information in this section on scrapers is excerpted from Sam Allen's *Wood Finisher's Handbook*.

It's a sad fact that scrapers have fallen into general disuse lately. Many new woodworkers have never seen or used one. Even though they may be hard to find, a good cabinet scraper and a hand scraper will be a wise investment for anyone serious about producing a topnotch finish.

It's important to keep a scraper sharp; a dull scraper doesn't work at all. A sharp scraper in the hands of an experienced worker can produce a surface so smooth that it's hard to duplicate even with very fine sandpaper. The procedure for sharpening a scraper seems a bit strange to someone who has never seen it done before, but once you've learned how, it's not hard.

In use, a scraper blade should have a slight bow sprung into it. With a hand scraper, you must bow the blade with your hands. Grasp the blade with both hands. Position your fingers around the edges, with your thumbs pressing against the middle of the blade. Press in with your thumbs to give the blade a slight bow. The bowed-out center of the blade should cut first; this means that you must push a hand scraper away from you, pushing mostly with your thumbs.

The scraper will produce a very thin shaving, not dust as sandpaper will. Always work the scraper with the grain. Overlap strokes as you proceed across the face of the board. As soon as the scraper shows signs of becoming dull, resharpen it.

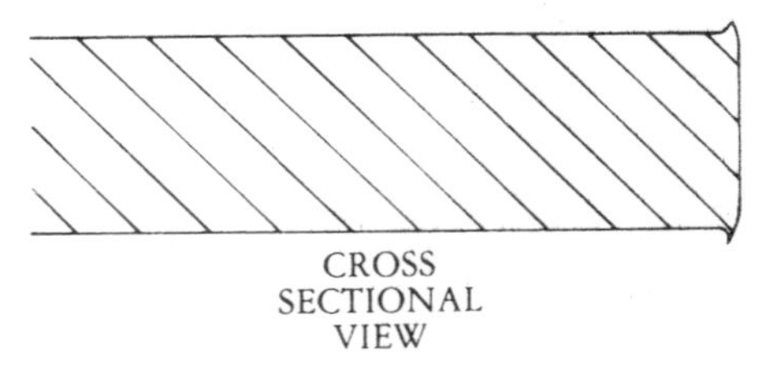

Cross-sectional view of a hand scraper blade.

The actual cutting edge of a scraper is a small burr that is formed on the edge of the blade. To prepare the blade to accept a new burr, place the blade in a vise whose jaws have been padded with wood blocks. Remove the old burr by filing across the face edge. Next, draw a smooth millfile across the edge, holding it perfectly flat and square on the hand scraper. Slightly round the corners. Next, use a whetstone to whet the edge. Hold the blade of the hand scraper square with the stone. Turn the blade on its side,

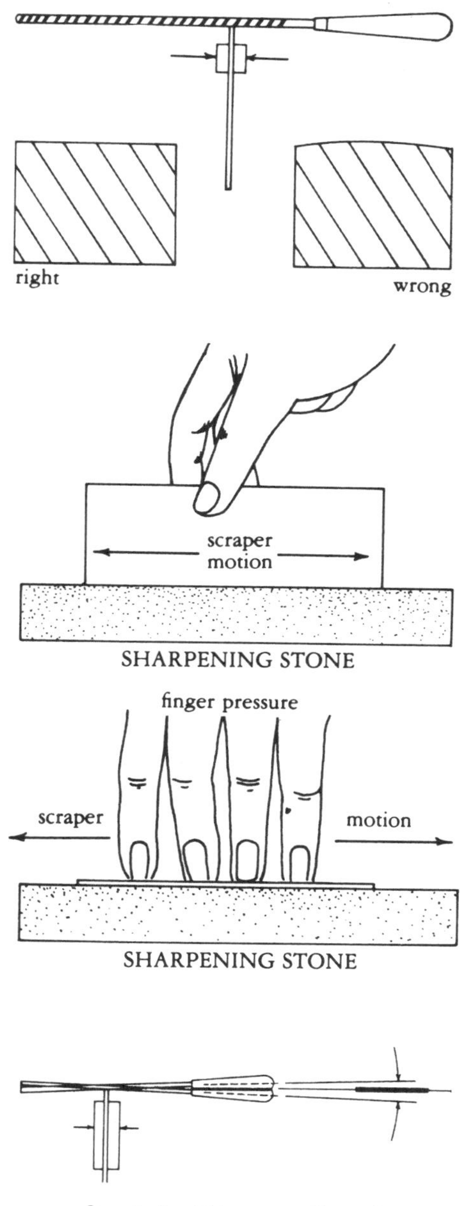

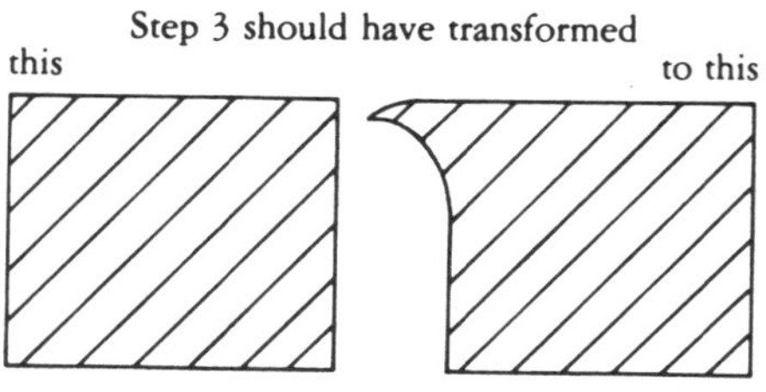

Step 1 in sharpening a scraper is to file the edge square. Whetting the edge on a sharpening stone is step 2. Forming the burr with a burnisher is step 3.

holding it flat against the surface of the stone, and rub it back and forth several times to remove the burr left from whetting the edge.

To form the cutting burr, you will need a burnisher. There are tools specifically made for this purpose, but any hardened tool steel object can be used. A lathe gouge or an awl will work well. Place the blade on a table with the cutting edge protruding about ½ inch past the table edge. Put a drop of oil on the burnisher and rub it over the entire surface. Holding the burnisher flat against the surface of the blade, draw it along the edge about four times. For the hand scraper, the next step is to position the burnisher so it is square with the face of the blade riding along the edge. Draw the burnisher toward you once and then tilt the burnisher slightly and draw it across the edge again. Take about three or four more strokes across the edge, tilting it a little more each time until the final stroke is made with the burnisher held at about 85 degrees to the face of the blade.

When the blade becomes dull, it is not necessary to file and whet the edge every time; simply repeat the burnishing process. When you can't get a good burr by burnishing alone, then file and whet the edge.

Scrapers also are useful for smoothing a shaped edge. You can purchase a ready-made scraper that is shaped so that different areas of the edge will fit the contours of various size coves. If there is a particular shaped edge (a roman ogee, for example) that you encounter frequently, you can grind one corner of a hand scraper to fit that shape. As you grind, take small cuts and keep the blade cool by frequently dipping it in water; otherwise, the blade will burn and lose its temper.

In the United States, woodworking and cabinetmaking are clearly defined trades; so is wood finishing. (*Vérisseur* [varnisher] is the French word for wood finisher. Not wishing to use this term because I rarely use varnish, I have had printed on my business cards the title *Technicien du Décor,* which describes my qualifications far better.) Theoretically, the cabinetmaker hands over his product to the finisher properly sanded with up to 150-grit sandpaper and ready to be finished. This rarely happens. The finisher is seldom satisfied with the quality of sanding. He knows that the smoother the wood, the easier his job of enhancing it with a finish will be. So, let's take a closer look at one of the finisher's most important tools: sandpaper.

Sandpaper is only about a hundred years old. Around the end of the 19th century in France, England, and Switzerland, woodworkers crushed glass into powder in mortars, strained it, and coated glue paper with the powdered glass, thus creating *papier de verre*, or glass paper. This technique was most likely practiced in other countries as well.

Prior to the advent of sandpaper, there were obviously other means to smooth wood. In the shop where I learned the trade in central Europe, it was difficult for us apprentices to lay our hands on costly sandpaper. We had to learn to sharpen our planes and scrapers to their sharpest, and to use the flats of our hands, instead of our eyes, to detect the slightest flaw on the surface of the wood.

Pumice was widely used in the shop. Pumice stone is a volcanic, igneous rock. In its natural state, it looks like a grayish-white sponge. This sponge-like texture is caused by water that comes into contact with the molten rock, and which is transformed into steam. The cooled rock becomes so porous that it can actually float on water.

The natural pumice was cut into blocks, one side of which was perfectly flat. This side was used much as a sanding block is used today, frequently with water as a lubricant. The powdered form of pumice was used the same way it is used today.

As a refinement, the pumice was pulverized, strained, graded, and compressed into blocks, with clay as the bonding agent. In the early twenties, we were still using these *bimsstein* bricks. In my school notes dating back to 1921, I had written the following: "The goal to polishing the wood is to eliminate all tool marks, to cut off the raised fibers, and to fill to some extent the exposed open pores of the wood. This is best accomplished with the *bimsstein* block, although some prefer using powdered *smirlgel* (corundum) or, on dark woods, powdered charcoal. Either of these could be used with water, oil, or tallow. Regardless, the operation has to be repeated three or four times at least."

I never used fish skin for sandpaper, but others did. In my notes, I found the name of the fish that provided this commodity—dornroche, a member of the ray family *(Raja elavata)*. Some sharkskin was, and maybe still is, used as an abrasive.

Old-time wood finishers had very few options regarding ways to make or improve the smoothness of wrought wood. They had to use nature-produced abrasives like garnet, pumice, sand (silica), and a few man-made ones like powdered glass, charcoal, and charred antler.

To this list, modern science has added new, sharper, far better abrasives, plus new and better ways to use them. Today, manufacturing abrasives is a huge industry. The technology of making abrasives can actually be considered a science.

Modern sandpaper consists of small abrasive particles coated on a sheet of backing paper. There are eight abrasives used in the manufacture of sandpaper. Five are man-made, and three are natural. Let's review them.

The natural abrasives are *flint*, *garnet*, and *emery*. Flint was one of the most common abrasives used in sandpaper years ago, but today it is difficult to find and rarely used. Most applications that call for flint paper can be done just as well or better with garnet, which is much harder than flint and, therefore, cuts much longer, or aluminum oxide, a man-made abrasive discussed below. In earlier days, flint was considered the best abrasive to use on soft woods. It does an excellent job of sanding off crumbling old finishes or paint. However, don't use it on quality work.

Emery is used primarily for cleaning metal, although it can be used on wood. It is harder than garnet, but because it doesn't fracture as easily, it won't renew its cutting surface like some of the other abrasives.

The five man-made abrasives are *aluminum oxide*, *silicon carbide*, *aluminum zirconia*, *industrial diamonds*, and *ceramic abrasives*. Aluminum oxide is sharp, tough, and widely used, deservedly. Some common trade names for aluminum-oxide paper are Adalox, Aloxite, Imperial, Metalite, Production, and Three-M-ite.

Silicon carbide, in my opinion, is the paper finishers should use—for two reasons. First, when the abrasive's sharp edge breaks off, the new edge is sharp also. Second, a variation of this abrasive is fused to waterproof backing, allowing wood finishers the luxury of wet sanding. Some common trade names for silicon carbide are Durite, Tri-M-ite, Fastcut, Powerkut, and Wet-or-Dry.

Aluminum zirconia is used to make fast-cutting and extremely durable sanding belts that are useful for removing old finishes and other heavy-duty sanding jobs. Industrial diamonds are rarely, if ever, used in wood finishing to achieve super-smoothness.

Ceramic abrasives are revolutionary proprietary minerals that exceed by far almost all the minerals presently in use. They are the most aggressive abrasives available. Extremely tough, they are also more expensive than the other abrasives. Because they are so aggressive, they are usually only used on coarse-grit sanding belts. Ceramic abrasives are a very good choice for shaping and removing a lot of wood. They are also useful for removing tough finishes. Some ceramic trade names are Cubitron, Norzon, Dynakut, and Regalite.

The hardness of these minerals is measured by two scales: the Knoop scale (1 to 8500) and the Mohs scale (1 to 10). The higher the rating, the harder the substance. Flint rates 820 on the Knoop scale and not quite 7 on the Mohs. Garnet is 1,360 on the Knoop scale, and about 8 on the Mohs scale. Aluminum oxide is 2050 on Knoop, 9.4 on Mohs. Silicon carbide is 2480 on Knoop, 9.6 on Mohs. Cubitron has a Knoop rating of 1600 and a Mohs rating of 8–9; more important, however, is its *toughness* rating, which, at 2.3, is almost twice that of aluminum oxide, which is rated at 1.2.

Modern sandpaper has backing that is versatile, and which fits perfectly the need for which it is designed. The backing for rough sandpaper is polyester cloth, graded XF or MF. The backing for micrograded minerals is polyester film. There are close to 20 grades and variations of backings between polyester cloth and polyester film.

Wood finishers have to be concerned with whether backing can be used wet or dry, or only dry. This information is given on each sheet of sandpaper. As long as they know this information, they should not be concerned about the bonds used to fuse these minerals to the backing. However, this information is also supplied with the sandpaper.

When the full surface of the backing is covered with mineral dust, the sandpaper is called "closed coat." When only 40 to 70% of the backing is covered, the sandpaper is called "open coat." Since each of the mineral grains that make up the sandpaper cuts (and is useful only as long as it is sharp), closed-coat sandpaper will cut more, last longer, and would generally be the better of the two except that it clogs up faster. On harder woods, I used closed-coat sandpaper; on softer woods, I use open-coat sandpaper. Open-coat sandpaper is also easier to clean.

The grading system of sandpaper is easy to understand. Actually, the size of the mineral grain used on the sandpaper determines its grit. There are several ways to designate grit size. The system most familiar to woodworkers in the United States is officially called the CAMI system. It uses standards set by the Coated Abrasives Manufacturing Institute (CAMI). In this system, the higher the number, the finer the grit.

The European abrasive grading system uses standards set by the Federation of European Producers Association (FEPA). It is called the P-scale. The P-scale has tighter tolerances than the CAMI scale, so the individual pieces of grit will be more uniform in size. In grades below 220, this isn't a major factor, but in finer grades used to polish finishes, more uniformity can result in few noticeable scratches.

The P-scale is similar to the CAMI scale until you get to grades finer than 220. P-scale grade numbers finer than 220 don't correspond to CAMI numbers. For example, the same grit size graded 600 in the CAMI system is graded 1200 in the P-scale. P-scale abrasives are labeled with a "P," followed by a number.

As an example of determining what grade of sandpaper to use on a project, imagine that you are covering a square-inch opening with a silk cloth that has 100 threads going from north to south, and 100 going from east to west, and that you are using this as a sieve to strain the mineral grain. The sandpaper that would be made with the mineral grain that goes through this sieve would be 100-grit sandpaper. If the screen has 200 threads going in each direction, the mineral dust strained would make 200-grit sandpaper.

Until not too long ago, the finest grit of sandpaper was 600-grit, which meant that when using the above-described method the wood finisher would have to strain the mineral grit through the 360,000 tiny openings the seive has (600 × 600). Several companies now make a type of sandpaper that is so smooth that one has a problem determining which is its rough side and which is its back. These micro-abrasive papers range from 1500 grit to 12,000 grit. Obviously, manufacturing a sieve with millions of openings over a square inch is impractical. Therefore, these micro-abrasives are graded using a flotation process that uses air or water to separate the particles by weight.

The worst thing you can do with sandpaper is rub one sheet against the other. If this is done with 100-grit sandpaper, you will not get two 200-grit papers, but two very dull, almost useless 100-grit papers. Use every bit of sandpaper while it is sharp, and throw it away when it is dull.

Sanding machines are rarely used by fine finishers. Sometimes orbital sanders, or "jitterbugs," can help you level built-up finishings between coats, and occasionally the orbital sander, or a rotary machine with a lamb–wool buffer, can help you with the final polishing-up. Whether you use these simple machines or do the sanding by hand, remember the following rule: Don't jump grits. For example, don't follow 80-grit with 280-grit sandpaper. Take your time and use more of the grits in between. Remember, when wood is smoother, not only is more of its beauty revealed, it is easier to finish.

Within the last decade, new abrasive devices have appeared on the market: micro-abrasives. These abrasives are a new way of making things smooth, and there is much to learn about them. They are gaining a foothold in the wood-finishing industry.

The micron system designates the size of the grit in microns (one thousandth of a millimeter). The micron system has even tighter tolerances than the P-scale system. This makes it desirable for polishing finishes.

The greek letter mu (μ) designates micron-graded abrasives. In this system, the larger the number the *coarser* the abrasive. In the micron system, 180μ corresponds to 80 in the CAMI system, and 15μ corresponds to 800 in the CAMI system.

In factories, micrograded belts are already smoothing and polishing films heaped on wood. Fine wood finishers can now accomplish the same results in a simpler way by using micro-mesh abrasives. These cushioned abrasive cloths can be used to produce a hand-rubbed shine that is smoother than that achieved via the traditional pumice and rottenstone methods. Micro-mesh cloth uses super-fine abrasives attached to a flexible cloth backing.

Micro-mesh abrasive cloth can be used dry or lubricated with water. Wrap it around a hard-foam rubbing block. The resilient latex bed that binds the abrasive allows the cloth to mold itself to the surface, so a uniform polish is produced over the entire surface.

Start polishing with 1500 grit and work through the grit until the desired polish is produced. Stop at 3600 grit for a satin finish or continue up through 12,000 grit for a high gloss. Most well-stocked finishing supply companies sell kits that include 9 grits from 1500 to 12,000 and a foam rubbing block.

The Norton company 3M and other companies market synthetic finishing pads, which are nonwoven nylon. These pads are sponge-like substances impregnated thoroughly with abrasive powders of various grits. These abrasives offer many advantages over sandpaper. They are flexible, waterproof (washable), nonloading, and don't tear easily. Furthermore, as old grain is used up, fresh grain is exposed. They seem to be the ideal product to polish shaped surfaces between coatings. I used them successfully to produce a satin finish after the last coats had dried. When it comes to odd shapes like moldings, carvings, or turnings, these abrasive "textiles" are the product wood finishers have dreamed about.

Synthetic finishing pads are a substitute for steel wool. They last longer than steel wool. They won't shed steel particles on the surface, and can be used with water-based finishes. They can be used in almost every instance where steel wool can be used.

Synthetic finishing pads come in several grades. The coarsest is called a stripping pad. It is equivalent to #0 steel wool. It is used to remove residue from the surface of wood when used with a chemical stripper. There are finer grades that are equivalent to #00, #000, and #0000 steel wool. Use the finer grades for smoothing a finished surface between coats.

If a finishing pad becomes clogged with finish residue, it can be washed out with water and reused after it dries.

Steel wool is an accepted, versatile tool that has many uses in the finishing shop. However, the future of steel wool as used in wood finishing does not look promising to me. When I inquired of a company about new steel-wool products it plans to introduce to wood finishing, I received the following reply: "We are not, nor have we ever been, involved in any research or development of new products for advances in steel wool." The abrasive textiles I've just mentioned will soon take over the better part of the steel-wool market, and rightly so. Many jobs that steel wool does, coated textiles can do better.

There are several possibilities about the ways abrasives will be used in the future. Perhaps they will be mixed in liquid, or maybe *bimsstein* will come back in some modern form. And, finally, let's not discard the possibility of micro-abrasives being fused to metal.

Finishing Products

Grease, oil, and wax, used four to five thousand years ago, were the earliest finishing materials. They are still being used today, although not for the same reasons. Our forefathers coated wood with oil, grease, tallow, or wax more to protect or preserve it than to improve its beauty.

Oils and Varnishes

Linseed oil is the best-known, and maybe the earliest, oil used in wood finishing. When applied on wood in thin layers, it absorbs oxygen, dries, and forms a light protective film on it. This oxidation, or more correctly, polymerization, is much too slow. Modern technology has produced "boiled" linseed oil, which dries much faster and meets the finisher's needs better. With "boiled" linseed oil, decent-looking, lasting finishes are produced that are easy to maintain or repair.

Tung oil is another excellent finish. It dries faster than boiled linseed oil and, more importantly, the film it produces is tougher, although it lacks luster.

Varnishes are the best finishes for protecting wood and improving its beauty simultaneously. Varnishes are combinations of oils and resins, and since both of these basic ingredients have countless variations, the possibilities of combinations are overwhelming. Some varnishes have several oils and resins.

Varnishes are classified into three main categories: oil varnishes, synthetic resin varnishes, and spirit varnishes. The most frequently used ingredients in oil varnishes are tung oil and linseed oil. Several varnishes also contain soybean or oiticica oils.

Oil varnishes can be subdivided into three categories according to the proportion of their oil content: short-, medium-, and long-oil varnishes. Of these three, the short-oil varnish is best for the fine-finisher. It compensates for the shortcomings of its protective qualities by the extreme hardness of the film it produces, and by the fact that it can be rubbed to a high gloss. Prior to the introduction of lacquer finishes, pianos were varnished with short-oil varnishes.

Long-oil varnishes are the best varnishes for outdoor work and for use on boats. They may not have as bright a shine as short-oil varnishes, but they resist "wear and tear" much better. Medium-oil varnishes, as the name indicates, have qualities that fall in between short- and long-oil varnishes.

Synthetic resin varnish is frequently called synthetic varnish. It is the most modern and versatile of the varnishes. A simple, man-made varnish, it can be used for any and all special needs. The best of the synthetic varnishes is polyurethane varnish, which can be used outdoors or indoors equally well, and gives good protection and an attractive look to the wood. The phenolic varnishes introduced in the 1980s are now being used for watercraft because they are durable.

Though varnish is a product that has been known for ages, modern varnish, which produces a beautiful coating, was introduced about two hundred years ago. The first of these varnishes had mostly spirits for solvents; oils were used later. The following information appeared in *Woodworker's Guide* in 1815: "In order to heighten the beauty of the fine wood and give additional luster to furniture, etc., it is the custom to varnish it. . . It is hardly worthwhile to make varnish as there are several shops where it may be had very good and at a fair price." This is still true. Varnish-making is a very involved process and is definitely not for amateurs.

Heated or not, slow-flowing or free-flowing varnish should be laid on wood evenly and skillfully, usually with brushes.

Dust is the greatest enemy of varnish. Here are a few "tricks of the trade" on how to fight it. Of course, I won't tell you to do all the varnishing in a clean shop that you have made as dustproof as possible, since this is self-evident, but I will tell you to avoid drafts or air currents that may carry dust.

I never dip my brush into the gallon can of varnish. With a ladle (that is made from a soft-drink or beer can), I take out as much varnish as I need and reseal my large container. I keep my brush spotlessly clean. My day container is a very clean tin can, across the top of which I fit a piece of wire (from a coat hanger). This helps me to squeeze out any extra varnish my brush may be holding.

Varnishes can be added to finishing oils or finishing oils can be used to thin varnishes. A finish with tung oil alone will produce a tough, protective shield on the wood, but it will be dull-looking. However, if you were to cover the wood with a mixture consisting of 10 or 15% glossy varnish and 90 or 85% tung oil, the mixture would dry to a semigloss shine. Such a mixture is actually "Danish" oil.

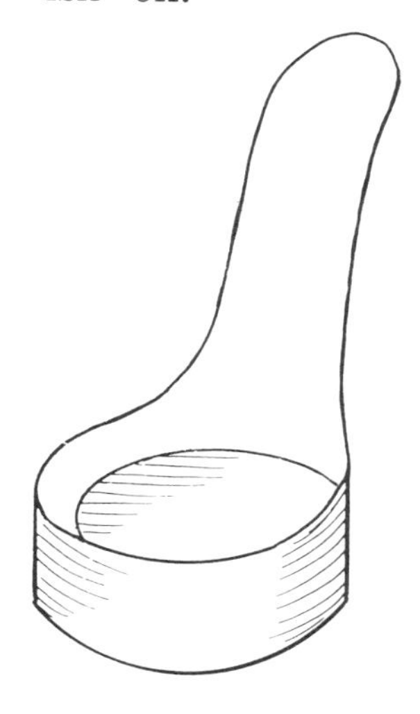

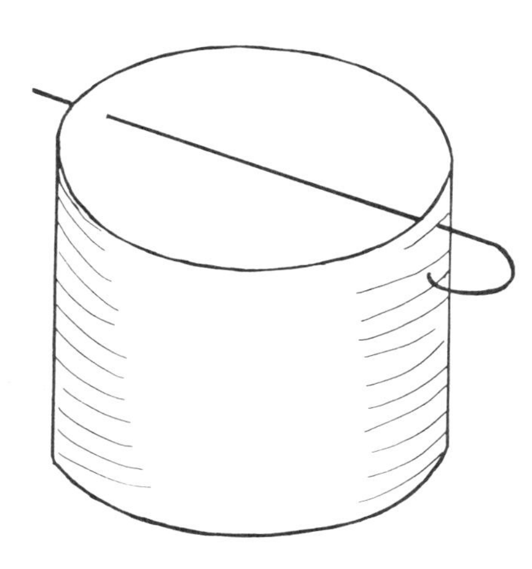

At left, ladle made from a beer can. At right, tin can in which varnish that is needed immediately is kept. Note the piece of wire on top, on which I wipe the brush.

Let's pursue this example of Danish oil. Combine a pint of "boiled" linseed oil with a half pint of spar varnish. In another container, dissolve one ounce of oil-soluble walnut dye in plain gasoline or mineral spirit. Mix the contents of the two containers thoroughly. The result is a walnut-color Danish oil that does not have to be shaken to be used. Danish oils that have to be shaken before use contain, besides an oil-soluble dye, a matching pigment.

Spirit Varnishes

Most of the spirit varnishes made out of gums are losing favor among fine-finishers. Few wood finishers know how to use or want to use gums like elemi, sandarac, manila, mastic, or dammar, although they are still a part of many specialty coatings such as picture protectors or instrument varnishes.

Shellac is by far the most important gum in this group. Many books define shellac as "a natural resin secreted by the insect *lacifer lacca* and deposited on the twigs of some trees in India."

This generally accepted definition of shellac—that the excrement from the insect is the shellac—may be a misleading one. According to my school notes from 1921: "Actually the tree covers the invading insect with a secretion, which when refined becomes the shellac."

Both descriptions of shellac are partially correct. According to A. F. Suter & Co., Ltd. (one of the world's leading shellac companies), the lac bug consumes resins exuded by the trees and processes the resins in its body to produce a hard, protective shell for itself and its young. This protective shell is the raw material for the shellac.

Shellac is the major ingredient in the best finishing method ever used: the French polishing discussed on pages 100–120.

Waxes

Waxes are extremely popular finishing products because for the amount of money and labor invested in a wax finish, you will receive the best buy in finishing. Waxes are easy to apply. Melted, they can be dissolved so as to jell into a paste or into a creamlike state. Since the carrier, or the solvent, is going to evaporate, the difference between the paste and a creamlike wax is that the paste wax will leave a heavier coating on the wood.

No matter which type is used, the wax will penetrate well into the pores of the wood and seal them effectively. It will provide strong resistance against moisture, fungi, dirt, and other finishes. Tricky craftsmen who reproduce antiques use paste waxes between layers of paint to make them peel. If you rub or brush the wax, it will acquire a soft, pleasant glow.

With aging, the soft, pleasant glow of wax can, and does, become a hard, burnished shine that is difficult to describe and more difficult to imitate. Waxes cannot be dissolved in water, but they can be emulsified with it, and emulsified waxes can produce this glow of age-burnished wax. However, these types of waxes are not as durable as some of the "older" waxes. The formula for emulsifying waxes is as follows: Melt four ounces of candella wax, four ounces of carnauba wax, and 6½ ounces of stearic acid in a double boiler. In a separate glass, earthenware, or enameled container, add one ounce of triethanolamine to 3½ quarts of boiling water. (If your tap water is high in minerals, use distilled water or rain water.) Now, pour the melted wax into the water; begin stirring with a wooden paddle as soon as you finish pouring. Continue stirring until the mixture cools and has the consistency of heavy cream.

Some paste waxes are much more expensive than others. In experiments I made, I compared these higher-priced waxes to my simple homemade wax, which consisted of plain beeswax, plus about 10–25% paraffin wax, dissolved in mineral spirit. I applied these waxes to wood samples and submitted the samples to torture tests: water, moisture, heat, and stains. The high-priced waxes turned out to be no better, nor worse, than mine—which cost a fraction of the price.

The waxes used in wood finishing are either produced by insects, like beeswax, or are derived from plants, like carnauba and candelilla wax, or are of mineral origins, like ceresin, ozokerite, and paraffin. These six waxes have basically the same properties; that is, they all are good water repellents, have smooth textures, have no unpleasant odor, and can be dissolved in most organic solvents.

Some books on finishing state that wax is not used on raw wood for finishing. This may be true now, but wax was frequently used on raw wood until the 1930s, and far later than that for finishing the insides of drawers and cabinets.

About fifty years ago, vegetable waxes were introduced as wood-finishing products. Carnauba wax, from Brazil, and candelilla wax, mostly from Mexico, are by far the hardest of these waxes. Both are marketed in several grades of refinement. The less refined they are, the more I like them. Rocklike, they respond to hard rubbing with a superior shine. I found out that this shine can be transferred to the wrought wood, and I incorporated both of these hard waxes in my water wax.

The harder the wax, the higher its melting point and shine. The approximate melting points for some waxes used in wood finishing are (degrees in Celsius): carnauba 85, candelilla 80, ceresin 70, and beeswax 60.

French Polishing

The great majority of wood finishers are poorly informed about French polishing, yet they are immensely interested in learning more about it. There are many trade books and magazines that discuss French polishing, but though they describe a finish that is produced with the same ingredients I use, the finish is not produced in the same *way*.

There is a great difference in the ways French polishing is practiced in France, England, Italy, and the United States. The methods that I shall describe are those that are practiced in France.

Ingredients

The ingredients used in French polishing are shellac, alcohol, oil, and pumice. Shellac, the most important one, is marketed in two different forms: flakes and liquid. To differentiate between the two forms, from now on I will refer in the text to the liquid form of shellac as "shelliq." (Editor's Note: The term "shelliq," coined by George Frank, is in the process of being accepted in more and more wood-finishing circles.)

I have always dissolved my own dry shellac because doing so gives me full control of the quality of the flakes and the proportions used in the solution. By doing this I am in essence producing my own shelliq. The single exception to this rule is white shelliq. Since shellac flakes are hard to preserve once they are bleached, I buy white shelliq each time I need some—and just enough to meet my needs.

Because shellac is used in many industries, its grading is rather complicated. I suggest that you use the selections I recommend, which are based on extensive experience. Purchase, if you can, Lemon No. 1 or Lemon No. 2 shellac flakes or superfine flakes. (Any commercial grade of blond or "superfine" shellac properly dissolved can produce a professional trouble-free job.) I have found very little difference among these three.

For dark wood, I dissolve garnet shellac. For very light wood, I either dissolve superblond flakes or use white shelliq that I buy ready-made.

Seedlac is a little-known member of the shellac family, and there is some confusion over the value of it in our trade. A booklet published by the U.S. Shellac Importers' Association contains the following information: "Seedlac is the natural product obtained by washing crushed sticklac. Shellac is the product obtained by refining seedlac."

It does not necessarily follow that a refined product is better than the unrefined version of it, or that shellac is better than seedlac for French polishing. I decided to experiment with seedlac. I purchased some, dissolved it in alcohol, and French-polished many objects with it. The conclusion I reached was that only sophisticated scientific instruments could detect any difference between seedlac and any other shellac that I have used in French polishing. Far more important than the degree of refinement in the shellac is the way a shellac finish is applied. A wood finisher can destroy a job with the "best" shellac or create a masterpiece with unrefined seedlac.

When one pound of dry shellac is dissolved in a gallon of alcohol, it is called a one-pound cut. If two pounds are dissolved, they are called a two-pound cut, etc. (This is a rather unprecise determination, since dry shellac has weight and volume. For example, if three pounds of dry shellac are dissolved in a gallon of alcohol, the result will be 1.3 gallons of three-pound-cut liquid shellac [shelliq], since a pound of shellac occupies a volume of 0.1 gallon.) This same system can be used metrically. If 250 or 350 grams of shellac are dissolved in a liter of alcohol (1000 grams), my label will read 250-gram-cut and 350-gram-cut shelliq.

Another important ingredient used in French polishing is alcohol. The best alcohol is ethyl alcohol, distilled from grain, but by law it is not allowed to be used in its pure form. Instead, C.D.A. (Completely Denatured Alcohol) is used. This is the solvent that I have been using for over sixty years in my French-polishing methods without any problems. Though there are several other shellac solvents available on the market, there is no reason to buy them because C.D.A. is the right solvent for shellac.

In my shop, shelliq is kept in dark bottles, and alcohol in light ones, not so much out of need as out of tradition. These two bottles are usually the same size and are kept close at hand, since they are used quite frequently. Both are corked, but the cork has a V-cut that allows the slow release of the content. A third bottle of 350-gram-cut shelliq is also kept nearby, along with a bottle of 350-gram-cut garnet shelliq, in case we are working on dark wood.

When not in use, keep alcohol and shelliq containers properly corked and stored away from heat. (Never store shelliq in metal containers.) If it is not properly corked, the alcohol will absorb some moisture, though probably not enough to interfere with the quality of the finish. Still, every finishing ingredient should be kept in meticulous condition. This may be the reason why in the sixty years I have practiced French polishing, I have never had to be concerned with the shelf life of dry or dissolved shellac.

Though oil is considered an ingredient in French polishing, it is not; it is merely an accessory. When tung or linseed oil is applied to wood, it becomes polymerized (oxidized), hardens, and forms a thin film on the wood. It actually becomes part of a finish-coating. Mineral oil in French polishing never becomes part of the finish. It simply helps to apply the finish when it lubricates the path the tampon runs over. In the end, as much of the oil is eliminated as possible.

Linseed oil, boiled or raw, is not used in the French method of French polishing. Instead, we use mineral oil or paraffin oil. Mineral oil is a petroleum derivative. It is available in two densities, light or heavy. I prefer to use the light one.

Pumice stone is an important ingredient in French polishing, and should be used in its finest grit, 4F. When we French-polished mahogany years ago, we used powdered red brick, which we made in a mortar, instead of pumice stone. Of course, we sifted it.

Though pumice powder is easy to spread over horizontal areas, it is more difficult to spread over vertical ones. The *couille*—a linen bag, about the size of a golf ball, that is loaded with pumice powder—is useful at this point. The *couille* reaches these vertical areas easily. Gently hit the areas with this device.

Couille, *a pumice dispenser.*

Tools and Accessories

In French polishing, a tampon is used to varnish the wood. The English equivalent of a tampon is the pad or rubber. The British fad is similar to the French *mèche*, which is either cotton waste or cheesecloth that is used on moldings, carvings, and other areas where the tampon cannot have proper access.

A tampon is basically a handful of knit wool taken from an object such as a sweater or socks, and contained in a "linenlike" cloth. This linenlike cloth can actually be made of cotton, nylon, or other material. Linen, however, is simply tougher than these materials and lasts longer. When I refer in the text to the cloth being used, I will call it linen, regardless of what it is actually made of.

The shape of the tampon is roughly that of an egg with one side flattened. The linen helps the tampon to assume and maintain such a shape. The linen fits tightly over the wool and helps the finisher squeeze and filter the wool's content as the tampon distributes it over the work. The correct ways of making the tampon into the proper shape and holding it are shown on pages 106 and 107 and explained in the captions.

A tampon is used to hold and release the shelliq according to the needs of the finisher using it. Once the woolen part of the tampon is "broken in," it should never be allowed to dry out, and should always be kept either in screw-lid jars or tin cans with tightly fitted covers called tampon cans. To break in the tampon, soak the knit wool with 250 shelliq and hang it out to dry. When it is half dry, store it away and later cut it into needed sizes.

Keep an assortment of 200-grit-and-higher sandpaper and two cardboard boxes nearby. Keep lint-free cheesecloth in one cardboard box, and an assortment of linen or linenlike cloths in the other.

True French polishing requires great pressure, and the object to be polished must be securely fastened to the workbench. Years ago each worker had his own assortment of tools, nails, cleats, and ingenious ways to fasten the job to the bench.

As I've mentioned earlier, the wood finisher today should have a basic tool kit. It should contain two hammers, various pliers, chisels, flat scrapers, screwdrivers, and nailsets, a block plane, and sanding blocks. He will add to the tool kit as the need arises.

Of course, brushes are needed to spread shellac. Years ago, I spread shellac with brushes made mostly of badger hair. They are costly, but with proper care they can last a very long time.

Two tools used years ago by wood finishers were the brass mortar, in which we reduced the oven-dried earth or the red brick into fine powder, and sieves, in which we sifted the powder to eliminate the rough particles. Though these tools are not used much today, they seem to be making a slow comeback. Both tools are in the catalogues of several suppliers. However, they are strictly for the amateur wood finisher.

Basics of French Polishing

If one ounce of shellac flakes is dissolved in five gallons of alcohol, and this thin solution is spread over an area of a thousand square feet, when the alcohol evaporates a very slight sheet of shellac will cover the whole area. If this experiment is repeated five more times over the same area, the result won't be six layers of shellac; instead, these six layers will combine to form one slight single layer. This attribute of shellac—to be able to be reduced into microscopically thin layers that fuse onto each other upon contact—is one of the keys to the superiority of this finish. The other key is the technique used, through which uncounted layers of such film can be spread on the wood.

In French polishing, the tampon does far more than just distribute the alcohol–shellac mixture over the wood. Through the pressure exerted from the finisher's hands, this mixture is forced into the pores and into all microscopic openings of the wood. To help the mixture fill the openings, the finisher will sprinkle, sparingly, some pumice powder on the wood; with the tampon, he forces the pumice powder into the pores.

As the pumice powder is being pushed into the pores, some of it gets stuck in the linen, and the linen, in effect, becomes a polishing cloth. This means that each time the finisher applies unmeasurably thin layers of a finish coating through an abrasive cloth, he smooths the surface from the beginning of the operation to the end. The smoothness achieved cannot be matched by any other finish.

There is another significant factor that is unique to this method: As the tampon is pressed down on the surface to grind the pumice powder into the pores, the pressure-propelled abrasive linen shears off microscopic rough particles of the wood and carries them into the pores, along with pumice and shellac. The wood is actually being filled mostly with its own substance.

Now that you are acquainted with the basics of French polishing, it is time that I teach you how to do it.

The best way to learn French polishing is to start with a relatively easy project. So, take a board of birch, beech, maple, or cherry about 16 × 20″, preferably ¾″ thick, and sandpaper it well, including all four edges. Nail two cleats underneath so that you will have easy access to the edges. Secure this board firmly to your workbench, and you are ready to begin.

First, wet the board with a damp, clean sponge. When it is dry, resand it with 220-grit sandpaper. Check the smoothness with your open hand, not just with your fingertips. Make sure your eyes are closed. Resand if not satisfied. Do all the edges well and don't leave sharp corners, but don't make them round, either.

Next, evenly and generously coat the board with clear, light mineral oil. Wipe off the excess oil with a paper towel. If the two ends have absorbed too much oil, they will be darker than the rest of the board. If this bothers you (it doesn't bother me), next time seal the ends with thinned-down glue, starch, or thin shelliq before spreading the oil.

From the tin can, take out the *broken-in* wool, cut off a piece, and form it in your hand to the shape and size of an egg. Put the remainder of the wool back into the tin can. Next, from the box where you keep the various sizes and kinds of linen, select one piece about 8 × 8″ that's fairly sturdy in texture, and wrap the wool tightly in it by pulling and twisting it over the wool. This combination of wool and linen is a tampon that should fit your hand snugly.

Wet the wool (which has been dried out halfway) once more with 250-gram-cut shelliq.

Now, hold the tampon in your hand so that all five of your fingers can be used if you want to squeeze it. About one-third of the tampon—the bottom of it—should be free from your grip. On this area the linen is stretched smooth; this is the area that will be in contact with the wood.

Next, take your bottle of alcohol and, without opening the linen, pour about a thimbleful of it throughout the bottom of the tampon,

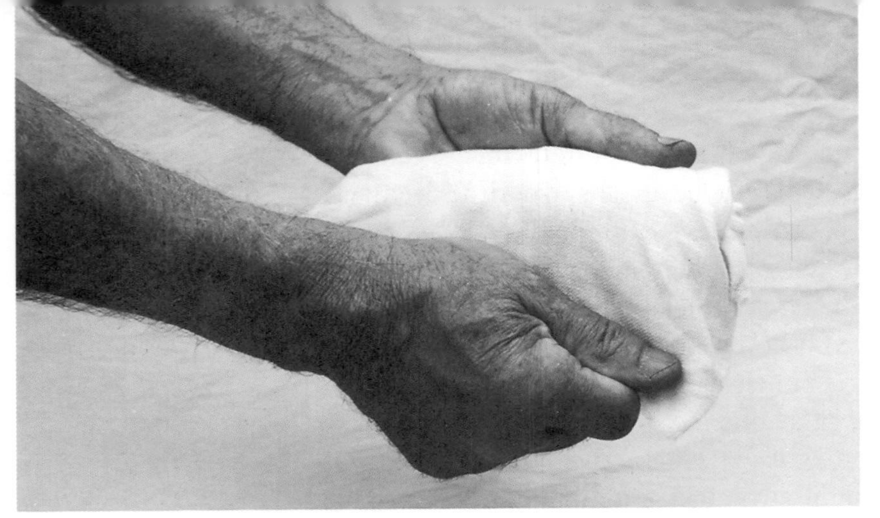

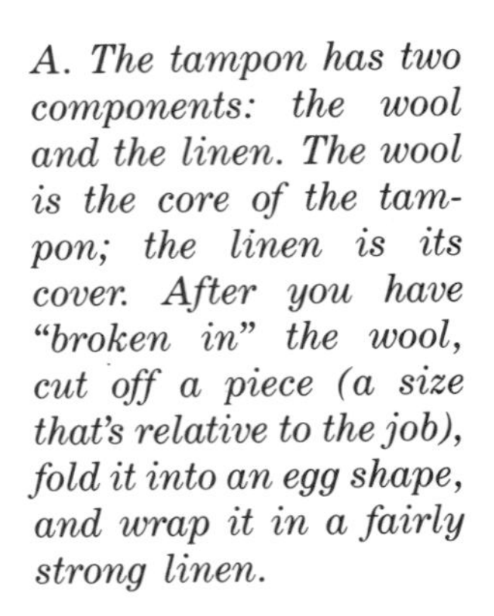

A. The tampon has two components: the wool and the linen. The wool is the core of the tampon; the linen is its cover. After you have "broken in" the wool, cut off a piece (a size that's relative to the job), fold it into an egg shape, and wrap it in a fairly strong linen.

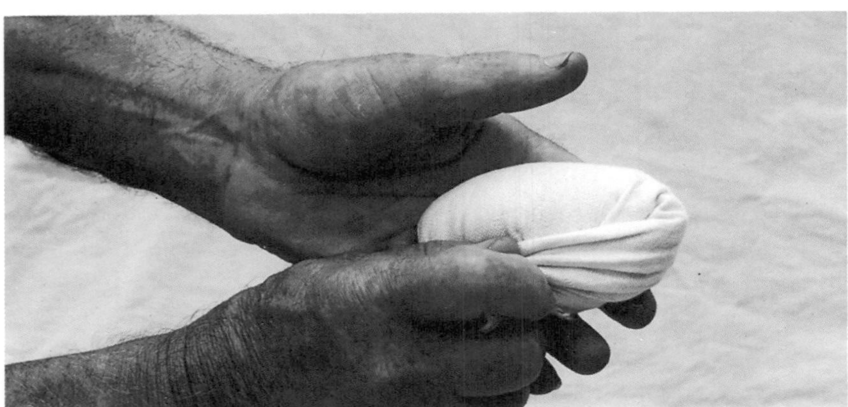

B. Next, twist the wool into the linen.

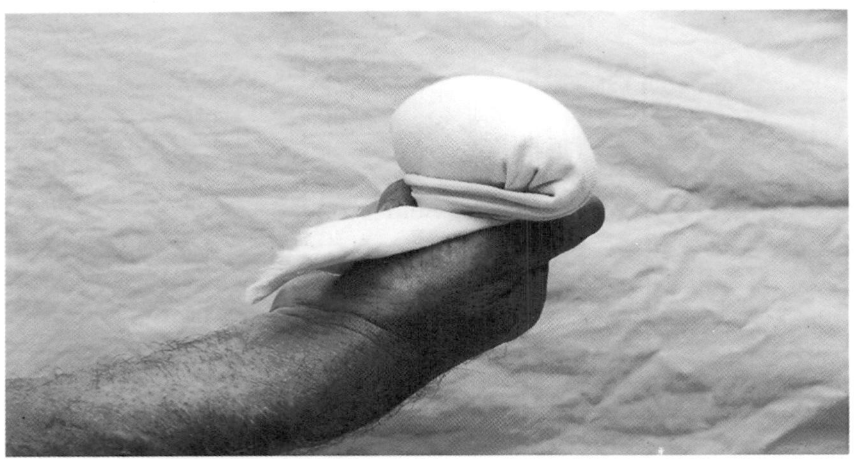

C and D. Pull the linen tightly over the wool.

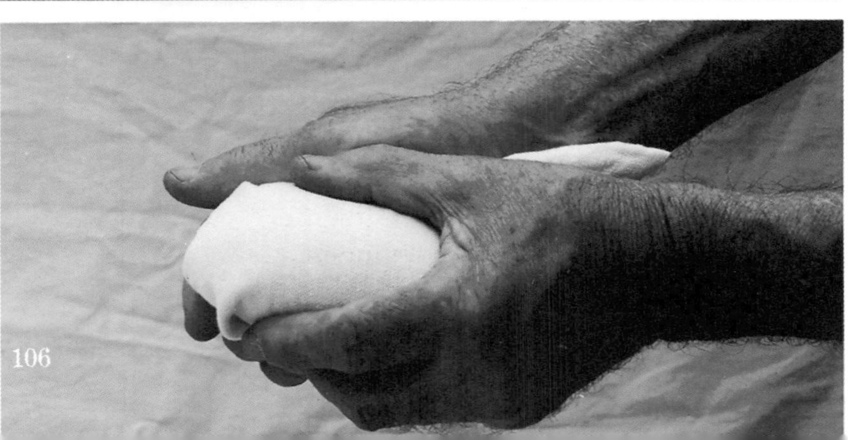

D.

E. The correct way to hold the tampon in your hands is shown here and in F and G.

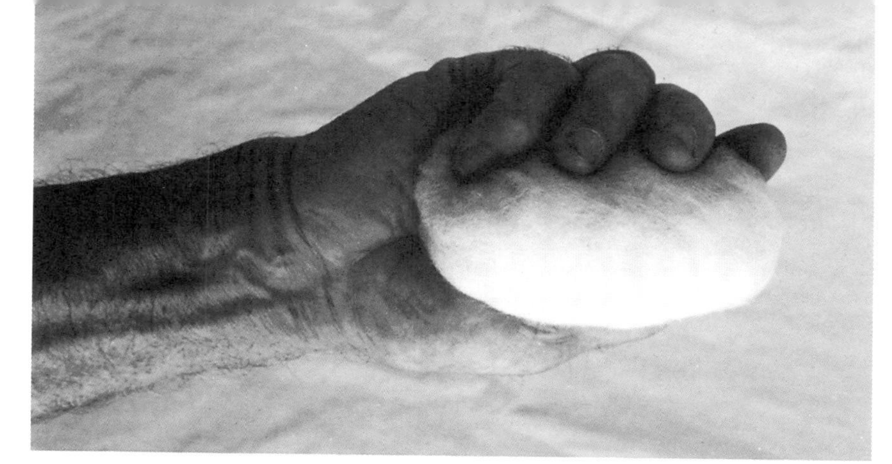

F.

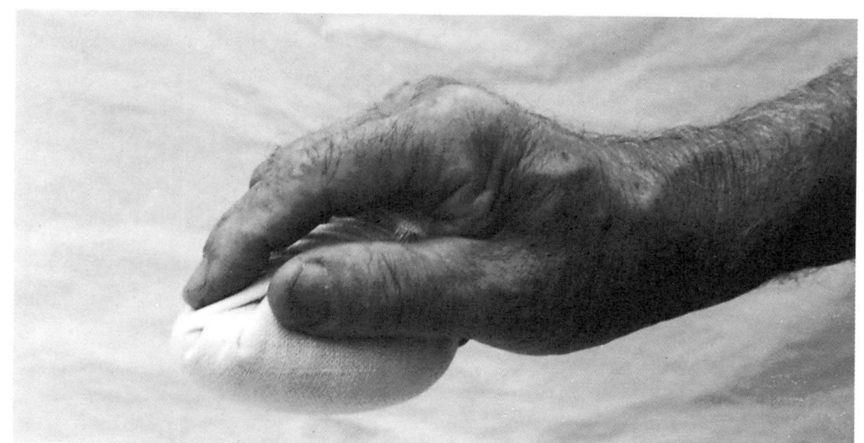

G.

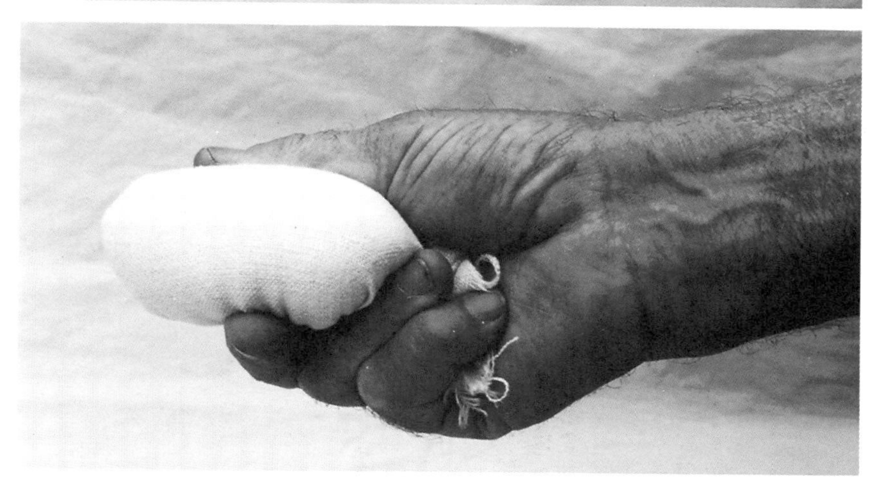

H. The tampon is now ready to be used on the project to be French-polished.

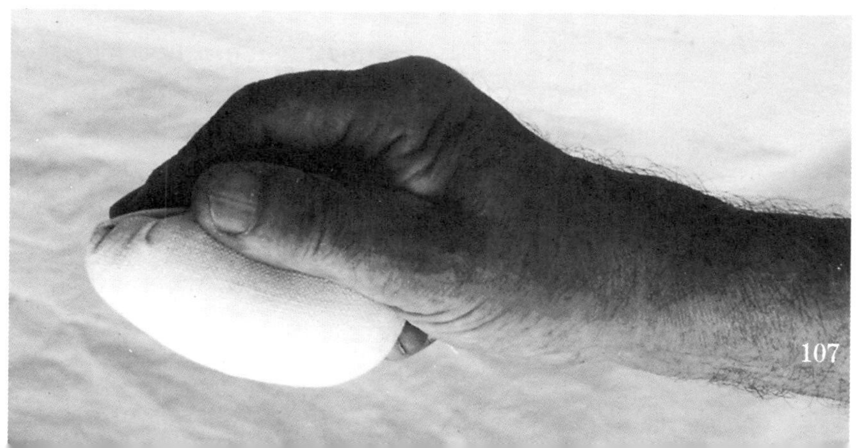

squeezing it every way so that the alcohol will be well distributed within. Sprinkle a pinch of pumice over the board and you are ready to French-polish.

Before beginning the polishing process, note that three factors determine the quality of the work: your coordination in squeezing the tampon when releasing its contents, the pressure of the tampon on the wood, and the way the tampon is moved over the job.

Begin polishing by pressing the tampon onto the board, simultaneously coating it with the shelliq and forcing the pumice into the pores of the wood. Always hold the tampon firmly in your hand.

Continuously move the tampon when it is in contact with the wood. *If you want or have to stop, lift up the tampon first.* The craft of wood finishing revolves around the pressure the finisher exerts upon the object being finished. This pressure ensures that the wood finisher will squeeze the last residue of shelliq–alcohol out of the tampon.

The tampon marks a broad ribbon on the surface. This ribbon should cover the surface evenly and frequently. To do this, you have to develop the right speed and rhythm, which is not hard to do. Note that when such a rhythm is achieved, you will actually be writing "words" like wou-wou and mou-mou on the surface. When you develop the proper speed and rhythm, remember that if you go over any area before the alcohol evaporates, then instead of adding a new layer over the old one you will probably wash off the previously laid ones. Also, remember that each passage of your tampon will leave a very thin coating on the wood.

Beginners have a tendency to neglect the corners and border areas. Do not make this mistake. Make a point of always moving the tampon over the corners and edges.

Stages

French polishing is generally performed in three stages, with an overnight drying period between each. The first stage is probably the most involved one. It includes the final sanding of the wood, sometimes the use of a filler and the sealing of it, and the oiling of the wood (including wiping off the excess).

To start the French polishing (details will follow), fill all pores and micro-openings and, when all this is accomplished, start the bodying. Let me elaborate on the filling of wood. Wood has pores, which are easily visible with the naked eye; it also has microscopic openings, scratches, and defects visible through powerful magnifiers. At the first stage of French polishing, we endeavor to fill all the visible pores of the wood as well as all the invisible imperfections. When this is properly achieved, the surface of the wood will be dressed in a smooth, uninterrupted sheet, and will be ready for the next operation: the "bodying." Bodying involves the use of almost measurable thick shellac coatings.

At the second stage, we look for any shortcomings in the board that occurred during the first stage. We fill the pores or openings that were missed, and when that is accomplished we continue the bodying.

We start the third stage—like the second one—by searching for any shortcomings on the board (there should not be too many at this stage) and then correcting them, finishing up the bodying, and clearing off the traces of oil remaining on the mirrorlike surface of our finish (the oil is by now so thin it is iridescent). This final operation is called "spiriting."

There is actually a fourth stage, in which we look at our work with admiration and a sense of pride and find someone to show it to. Modestly, we accept his or her compliments.

General Notes on the First Stage

When we start the first stage, all pores on the board are filled with oil, but as these pores fill with pumice powder the oil is forced out. It goes to the surface. As the thickness of the shellac increases on the surface, the tampon will not slide as easily as it did earlier. The oil that is forced out of the pores becomes part of a needed lubricant.

At this point, check that all pores on the board are properly filled, that pumice is not gathered in small heaps, and that your work is satisfactory. (One thing should be pointed out here: Proper light is an absolute necessity when French-polishing, since at all times you must be aware of your progress. You should be able to determine the slightest imperfection on your wood. Either position your work so that it reflects a source of light or position the light so that you can see it reflected in your work.)

French polishing has one simple rule: If anything goes wrong with the job, you can correct it with alcohol. One exception to this rule occurs with pumice heaps. Beginners have a tendency to use too much pumice, and end up with these heaps. They have to be eliminated with the use of 600-grit wet-and-dry sandpaper, very little water, and a lot of care. For such a job, I use a small sanding block—a 2 × 3-inch piece of marble (a hardwood block will also do). The heap eliminated, feed your tampon with alcohol and keep working until the whole board presents a well-filled, unbroken, even surface. Now, you are ready to begin the bodying.

Up until now, you have fed your tampon only alcohol. Now, you will use shelliq 250. To feed the tampon with alcohol, you poured it on the bottom of the tampon, without taking the linen off. To feed it with shelliq, lift up the linen and pour the alcohol onto the wool, and the shelliq on top of the alcohol. When the tampon is squeezed, the two ingredients are mixed and distributed within it.

At any feeding, the quantity of shelliq should never exceed that of the alcohol. At this first feeding, for each part of shelliq 250 add two to three parts of alcohol. At successive feedings, slowly increase the proportion of shelliq, but never exceed the half-and-half ratio.

With the tampon gradually carrying more and more shelliq, you will find yourself writing longer U's and 8's on your board. Adjust the way you squeeze, and press down on the tampon to compensate for its wetness and moisture. Exert little pressure on a freshly loaded tampon, and a great deal of pressure on a nearly empty one.

As the tampon unloads a new layer of thin coating at each passage, and as each of these new layers is added to the thickness of the finish on the wood, you will notice that the tampon doesn't slide on the wood as freely as it once did, although you have forced out the last drop of oil from the pores of the wood. It is now time to use droplets of mineral oil as a lubricant. Mineral oil is good to use because it doesn't harden, doesn't form a film, and doesn't become part of the shellac finish.

British, Italian, and American finishers differ from French finishers in that they use linseed oil quite generously. However, they also use far more and heavier shellac coatings than the French, and it's possible that the oil somehow becomes part of such a coating. The French way, in my opinion, produces a finer, thinner, and far tougher finish.

Assuming that your board is well filled, that it is coated with a thin coat of shellac, and that you have been releasing more of the shelliq 250 gently from your tampon, you will notice that the passage of the tampon leaves an oily mark. These marks are called "clouds"; the quality of these clouds indicates how your work is progressing.

When the pores of the wood are filled and you are about to start the bodying, the tampon will need lubrication. Mineral oil, used very sparingly, provides such lubrication. While the tampon leaves layers of shellac on the wood, the oil remains on the surface and forms "clouds." From this point on, until the very end, the clouds must be present, since they indicate that everything is going well. At the final stage, they will be eliminated through a process called spiriting. (Editor's Note: Traces of clouds can be seen in the photo; they are very difficult to photograph.)

As you slide your tampon over the board, you will clearly see the alcohol evaporating; its passage is marked by these clouds. The production of "healthy" clouds is a good sign; the production of "poor" clouds is a bad sign. The differences between "healthy" and "poor" clouds are very difficult to describe, and it is better to show them. (See photo above.) The remedy for poor clouds, as for almost every problem in French polishing, is the use of alcohol.

To simplify your introduction to the practice of French polishing, we are using in this example a non-dyed wood. Let's examine the differences in the finishing processes if we were instead to use a board that had been dyed to a medium-brown color with a water-soluble aniline dye. The main difference is that at the first stage, before using any pumice powder, we must protect the new artificial color of the wood. So the finisher must feed his tampon with shelliq 250 and, following the grain, put a good protective coating on the board before starting to use pumice, sparingly.

By now your tampon has adapted to the shape of your hand, and should fit there snugly. The bottom of the tampon—the part that slides on the wood—should be clean. If not, feed it with alcohol until it is.

Your wood should now be well filled, and behind the clouds you should easily see the beginning of a beautiful finish. All that's needed to complete the first stage is for you to do the edges.

As I've already mentioned, shellac's most amazing quality is the immediate fusion of its layers. This quality is the key to the finishing of areas impossible to reach with a tampon, like an elaborate carving, a complicated molding, or the four edges of your board. To do the edges, use shelliq 350 (a heavier solution). From cheesecloth about 20 inches square, make a flat pad (British fad or French *mèche*), load it with shelliq (no alcohol), and, immediately at the beginning of the first stage, coat the edges with it; then place the pad in your tampon box.

Every five minutes or so repeat this operation; in between coats, use whatever abrasives the job allows for (in this case, high-grit sandpaper) and go over the edges with the tampon also. By the time the board is ready, so will be the edges. However, while the top of the board will be French-polished, the edges will merely be finished with shellac. The difference will not be that noticeable.

While you have applied practically hundreds of thin layers of shellac to the top of your board, you have only applied a dozen or so heavy coats to the edges. Heavy coats of shellac have the tendency to become cloudy and blurred, and hide, to some extent, the markings of the wood. To prevent this muddiness on these heavily coated areas, I use quite frequently a special shelliq that is my 350-gram-shellac mixture filtered through a double layer of cloth.

General Notes on the Second Stage

The board should be securely fastened to your bench and should be well illuminated. Examine it thoroughly. You may find, for example, that the southwestern area is not as smooth as the remainder of the board, and that, in fact, there are unfilled pores. This is easy to correct. Repeat a shortened version of the procedures used in the first stage. With alcohol and pumice (reduced quantities of each), refill the pores, paying attention mostly to the neglected areas.

Feed the tampon with alcohol alone and the "healthy" clouds will reappear, signaling that you can now return to the bodying. Again, slowly increase the shelliq content of the tampon, never going over the 50–50 ratio; make sure that the bottom of the tampon is clean, and look for the clouds. If they do not appear, something is wrong. If everything goes well, you will detect under the healthy clouds a superb gloss unmatched by any other finish.

Up until now, you have occasionally been using dabs of oil and traces of pumice. Pumice at this stage no longer fills the pores, but is used as part of the linen to rub and to polish the surface.

Now you are reaching the end of the second stage. Feed the tampon with alcohol alone and use up its contents by drawing huge 8's on the board from one end to the other. By the time your tampon is dry, you will be fully satisfied with the work. Make sure you do the edges the same way you did them in the first stage.

General Notes on the Third Stage

First, examine the work so far, looking for any problems and imperfections. If there are any, correct them.

The board being used here is merely a sample. However, if it were a job—a tabletop or door—you would have to coat the back of it with two coats of heavy-cut shelliq applied with a brush to seal the pores and prevent warping. (One of the greatest problems in woodworking is preventing the warping of wood. The most accepted measure of protection is to coat both sides of any board to obstruct the access of moisture into the unfinished area.) A cabinet door must be finished on both sides, though not necessarily with the same grade of finish, and a quality tabletop must also be coated on its underside, regardless of whether it is exposed or not.

The edges have to be finished before you can finish the top. At this stage, they are well coated and acceptably smooth. This smoothness was accomplished as you sandpapered the edges constantly with finer and finer paper, and when you went over them frequently with the tampon. However, the finish on the edges is not as good as that on the main area. The edges are not ready to be "spirited."

About sixty years ago, at this stage I would have applied on the edges a coating of "copal," a spirit-varnish that dries to a cheap-looking finish and is difficult to work with. I have since replaced the copal with 350-gram-cut shelliq that is filtered through the kind of paper filter used in coffee makers. Shelliq filtered in such a way is clear, almost transparent, and easy to work with.

I carry in my shop foam rubber salvaged from old pillows or cutoffs bought from upholsterers. It has many uses in the finishing shop. To apply my filtered shelliq 350, I cut a piece of the foam rubber about a cubic inch, wet it well with the filtered shelliq, and coat the edges easily and evenly. The advantages of this method are that I can repeat the procedures if not satisfied and can go over the job with my tampon or my pad of cheesecloth—a great improvement over the "copal"-coating method.

Now, you are ready to concentrate again on the finish of the top. Remember that this, the third stage, is the final one. Assuming that you have checked and corrected any problems you may have had, continue the bodying but no longer use pumice powder and use oil very sparingly, since, as you go, you will have to eliminate the oil that clouds up the mirrorlike finish.

Change the linen on your tampon, this time using a lighter one; you will gradually diminish the proportion of shelliq as you feed the tampon. Before each feeding use up all moisture in the tampon, using the proper pressure. The healthy clouds have to be present, except that by now they are becoming thinner and thinner and are slowly becoming iridescent. The last feeding of your tampon should be with alcohol alone, and not too much of it. If properly done, the clouds (always present) should be by this time very thin and really iridescent. If not, repeat the alcohol feeding. Dry out your tampon using long, neat strokes, and when it is dry put it away in your tampon can. You are ready for the spiriting.

Now, change the tampon. Take out a new one that has never contained shellac, pumice, or oil. Dress it in clean, soft linen and add alcohol to it. Don't rub the finish with it; gently move it over the finish. This will help you eliminate all oil remaining on the board. In addition, sprinkle Tripoli earth on the finish. It is a superfine abrasive, and will absorb some of the oil.

"Imitation" French Polishing

While French polishing can be easily done on large, flat surfaces, it is frequently impossible to French-polish carvings, moldings, turnings, etc. On such areas, finishers do an imitation of true French polishing—a procedure that nearly all manuals erroneously describe as true French polishing. Here the thickness of the film is built up, and the coating leveled between applications with various abrasive tools. In *true French polishing*, the abrasive tool, the tampon, is the applicator.

In "imitation" French polishing, which is merely a shellac finish, the shellac or shelliq is applied in a simpler way. There is no attempt to grind pumice into the pores of the wood. The tampon is no longer used somewhat like sandpaper. Instead, the finisher heaps coats upon coats of shellac on the shaped object; between coats, he uses all available means to make them as smooth and even as possible.

In imitation French polishing, tampons cannot be used effectively. Instead, shelliq 350, the heavier solution, is applied either with badger brushes or with the best tampon substitute, the "mesh," which is plain, lintless cheesecloth that can be easily adapted to fit any shape that needs to be coated.

Since the finisher is working with far heavier layers of shellac, the drying time is longer, and it must be observed. After three, four, or five repeated coatings, the wood finisher must stop and even up or smooth the finish. Sandpaper, preferably the no-fill type, can be used to do this. Steel wool is an old standby that's also acceptable, but there are now products that can be used that are better, such as abrasive-coated textiles like Bear-Tex®.

Of course, carved areas can also be smoothed with stiff scrubbing brushes, if the finisher has a lot of patience. Still, the best smoothing tool is the "mesh," which carries the shelliq to the surface.

Though with mesh you must use more oil and less alcohol, it is a smoothing tool that can bring up a shine similar to that achieved through real French polishing. The key is to reduce the quantity of feed and to increase the pressure.

Spiriting cannot be used on this type of shellac finish. However, I have found an adequate substitute. See page 114 for a description of filtered shelliq 350 and ways to use it.

Open-Pore French Polishing

As I have just discussed, there is a difference between French polishing and a shellac finish. True French polishing centers around the following: the grinding of pumice into the wood, the continuous rubbing-polishing with the pumice-laden linen, and the pressure needed for these techniques. In a shellac finish, these techniques are not needed. True French polishing uses little shellac but spreads it over large areas under great pressure; in a shellac finish, fewer coatings are used, but they are heavier, and there is less rubbing and, of course, pressure.

There is, however, at least one exception to this generalization of French polishing. During the first twenty-five years of this century, many outstanding pieces were finished through open-pore French polishing. This type of finish was practiced mostly on wood with large pores, such as oak, chestnut, and ash. The pores were left unfilled or only partly filled, and their markings were easy to read and attractive.

In 1921, I was part of a team working on the furnishings of an elegant mansion. Three adjoining rooms were paneled with selected oak. The oak in all three rooms was of matching lines and designs, except that one was dyed black, one left natural, and one (the smoking room) was obviously fumed oak. All three were finished through open-pore French polishing and, even by today's standards, were handsome and elegant.

Using scrapers, *bimssteins*, sandpaper, and repeated wet sanding, we made the wood as smooth as possible before starting to French-polish the open-pore way. We did not use oil or pumice stone, but we did use pressure and hard rubbing. We unloaded the contents of our tampon by drawing huge 8's on the boards, and laid a large number of extremely thin coats on the boards until the coats dressed the wood in a silk-like finish that can only come from French polishing.

Beginners should also use this technique. Start easy, don't overfeed the tampon, and allow time for the layers to dry before applying the next coat. Spend some time practicing this technique, and you will find it ideal.

Variations of French Polishing

For at least a half century there has been a search for ways to imitate, simplify, or replace French polishing. For example, in Paris in the 1930s, experimental machines were developed to replace or to help the *vernisseur* (wood finisher), in which three tampons were used to whirl on the wood. These machines were unsuccessful. Variations on them were offered to me on two separate occasions, but I did not "buy" the idea.

Lacquers

The relationship between chemistry and wood finishing is similar to that between mother and child. Elementary chemistry has taught wood finishers about the protective and decorative values of oils, waxes, and gums; progressive chemistry has taught us about dyes we can extract from plants or refine from coal tar, and has shown us the incredible potential of shellac.

During World War I, nitrocellulose was the prime material used in the making of explosives and other destructive devices. At the end of the war, the fighting nations had a huge stockpile of the material. The science of chemistry made lacquer out of nitrocellulose, and the destructive compound became the prime material in the most important finishing product of our time. To some extent, the biblical prediction—that swords will be made into plowshares—was fulfilled.

Lacquers are versatile and tough. Lacquer finish is far easier to produce than French polish, yet its shine and clear transparency are very similar to that of French polish. The protection the lacquer finish offers is far greater than that of the French polish. Apparently, the lacquer finish is superior in many respects, except that it lacks that hard-to-define quality—*je ne sais quoi* (I don't know what)—of the classic French polish.

In my New York factory, at least 90% of our work was finished with laquer. Still, I feel that as far as lacquer finishes are concerned, you can easily find teachers who are better qualified than I am. Abundant information is available not only in books and magazines but also from nearly all major suppliers, who will help you to select the proper variety of lacquer finishes for your needs.

The home craftsman is somewhat handicapped when working with lacquer finishes, since he needs compressed air and good ventilation (ideally, a spray booth). Sometime in the early 1980s a new type of compressor and spray-gun combination called HVLP was offered to the finishing trade that solved both of these problems. Presently, several variations are on the market. According to my information, the two most important ones go under the names of Apollo and Croix. I cannot tell which one is better for our needs or which is the better buy, but I can tell you that I own the Croix spraying system and not only am I satisfied, I can also vouch for the accuracy of the information put out by the manufacturer, which reads as follows:

* Up to 50% savings in material
* Up to 80% reduction in overspray
* Portable—No compressor needed
* Low maintenance—easy cleanup
* Clean, healthier spraying environment
* Continuous supply of dry, oil-free warm air
* Use a gun with cup or pressurized paint tank
* Solves humidity blushing problems

In the small shop where I mostly do experimental work, my Croix spraying system is a blessing. I have no compressor, spray booth, or exhaust system, and rarely have to use a mask.

High-Volume Low-Pressure (HVLP) spray systems use low-pressure compressed air to atomize and propel the liquid. Because the liquid is traveling at a slower speed, 65 to 90% of it stays on the surface.

HVLP guns can be operated from conventional air compressors, but for small shops and home use, a turbine-driven HVLP gun is an attractive alternative. You can buy a complete system for less than the cost of a conventional compressor. The turbine works like the exhaust of a shop vacuum, except that the turbine is more powerful.

These HVLP spraying systems are invaluable in the shop of the fine-finisher, but there are additional ways that lacquers can be applied to wood. I do not have the necessary experience to give advice on the use of the airless spray gun, but I do have practical experience with two others: brushing and padding lacquers.

Brushing Lacquers

In July 1987, I visited several woodworking shops in China where lacquering was performed. From a supplier I ordered the ingredients needed to produce the famous Chinese lacquer, and with the help of a team of other dedicated wood finishers, I intend to study, evaluate, and master this craft, which has been practiced in the Orient for thousands of years. Evidently, the Chinese lacquer is applied by brushes that have been perfected over many centuries; I am convinced that they represent a key factor in the craft. Like the brushes we use, these brushes come in many widths ranging from one to four inches. Strangely, I have rarely seen a worker using a brush other than the four-inch brush. These brushes are not costly in China, and I hope that you will soon be able to purchase them in America also; with them, you will be able to apply our excellent American lacquers without any problems. There are several lacquers on the market specially formulated for brush application.

While visiting China, I noticed that in its factories lacquer is not sprayed on, it is brushed on.

Padding Lacquers

If French polishing and lacquer were to marry, their offspring would be the padding lacquers. My evaluation of these lacquers could well be biased, since I was brought up with a tampon in my hand and in my heyday felt that I could beat any other method of finishing wood.

About thirteen years ago, I received from the leading manufacturer of these padding lacquers, H. Behlen and Bros., a generous quantity of nearly every product they were marketing in this line. After some experimentation, I concluded that these lacquers were good, but whatever they could do I could do better with my shelliq and tampon. This conclusion was confirmed by my good friend Thomas W. Newman, an excellent restorer in Hoboken, New Jersey. Our assessments of these padding lacquers were close. Mine was based on superficial experimenting, and Thomas's experiment was conducted merely to determine if it would lead to the same results.

However, the more I have worked with these padding lacquers, the more convinced I have become of their excellent quality and usefulness in the fine-craftsman's hands. My friend also endorses them more enthusiastically now. His opinion is based on daily use of these lacquers, and it should be respected more than mine.

Padding lacquers are unbeatable in the repairing, refinishing, and restoring trades. The only reservation I have about using them is that they are marketed in too many variations, which makes it confusing to use them.

Milestones in Wood Finishing

If you were to look at a wooden board through a microscope, you would see that although the wood might feel smooth and flat, it would, in reality, have pores, and its surface would be rough. In the chapter on French polishing, we ground pumice into the pores of the boards we experimented on. This pumice, combined with shellac and microscopic wood fibers, filled the pores. There are several alternate techniques that will instead *highlight* the pores and transform them into a decorative element.

Filling Wood Pores Decoratively

Early in my career, I discovered that I had the ability to dye wood with deep, penetrating colors. The technique I used consisted of filling the pores of tinted or naturally dark-colored wood with a distinctly different-colored filler, only for decorative purposes. This process had been mentioned to my classmates and myself by an elderly professor years before. He never actually demonstrated the technique to us, or showed samples of it, yet, somehow, the idea remained deeply engraved in my memory.

In an attempt to master this technique, I spent month after month during my leisure time experimenting with wood. By the time I reached my 24th birthday, I had completed two sets of 15 samples.

My 15 samples all had clean, crisply defined colors, with either contrasting-color fillers or a "tone-on-tone" combination, where wood and filler are the same color but of different intensities. All these vibrant colors were dressed in a faultless French-polished gloss.

Jansen, Inc., was at the time the most prestigious interior decorator in Paris, and probably in the world. By sheer luck, all three of its directors—Schwartz, Vandries, and Boudin—were present when I presented my samples at Jansen. Incredibly, I was hired on the spot as foreman of the finishing department, and eighteen months later, with Jansen's financial backing, I started my own woodworking business.

Totally inexperienced in business matters, I invested my meager working capital in designing, making, and finishing a highly luxurious dining-room suite. I decided to use my pore-highlighting technique, unaware that its cost would drive me to near-bankruptcy.

In my desperate situation, luck once again smiled on me. I managed to rent a store window in the very heart of Paris, where I exhibited my dining room. Through the kindness of the store owner, I was able to borrow a large Persian rug, good paintings, and accessories that complemented the furniture. The suite appeared in all its splendor. And splendid it was! The design was pure Art Deco, with rather simplified clean lines. The wood was selected oak; its veneered areas were perfectly jointed and book-matched. Everything was geared to bring out the beauty of the finish.

Let me describe step by step the technique I used to finish this dining room. Since most of the areas had been veneered, my first job was to remove from the pores of the veneer the hide glue that had been used in the veneering. I soaked these areas with warm water, sponged off the excess and, while the wood was still moist, cleaned the pores with a clean, soft wire brush. (Wire brushes are the wood finisher's best friend.)

I made the black dye using logwood extract, topped with a homemade chemical that consisted of a vinegar–iron combination (see page 23). I used the logwood extract and the homemade chemical in warm, concentrated solutions and, for good measure, repeated the applications, preceding each one with sanding and dusting.

Next, I protected the positive, deep-black color of these smooth surfaces with a substantial coating of open-pore French polishing, followed by the filling of the pores. I filled the pores with alabaster, the "plaster of Paris" used by sculptors and artists. I mixed this fine powder with ultramarine dry color, approximately half and half, in a large enough quantity for the whole job. I used two flat dishes, one to hold water and another to hold the blue powder. With a folded piece of soft cloth dampened with water, I picked up some blue powder and, while it was wet, rubbed it into the pores; I cleaned the excess before it hardened. It was a long, tedious job, but worthwhile, since it filled each and every pore entirely without shrinking.

The next day, I very carefully perfected the cleaning, using fine sandpaper and steel wool, so that the black areas were black and the pores neat, clean, blue, and distinct.

The next step was the French polishing, which turned out to be the most difficult French polishing job I have ever done. The wood had to be coated heavily with shellac before I could use "hints" of pumice. It took more than a month of working 60–70 hours per week to finish this dining-room set. Today, with modern tools and spray equipment, I could do the same job in a fourth of the time. This blue dining room was the only project in which I did a complete, high-gloss French polishing job over decoratively filled wood.

Though tourists did not notice my blue dining-room exhibition—including my 15 samples in the foreground—tradesmen did. Within days I had far more work than I could handle. Within weeks my dining room was sold and my financial situation looked better. I had a winner on hand.

I do not claim or pretend that I invented the process of decoratively filling pores but, because I was faced with an onslaught of projects in which this technique was being used, I had to, and did, invent a simpler way to achieve the same effect.

In simplifying the method, I did not give up the wetting and wire-brushing of all veneered surfaces, but I did replace the old-fashioned dyes with aniline dyes, imported from Germany (Arti Dyes) and, more importantly, I replaced the filler with the kind of filler that was easy to use and fast to clean.

The new filler was plain chalk powder mixed with the needed dry color, which served as the pigment. The carrier was plain gasoline; the binder was a mixture of melted beeswax and paraffin wax. This filler entered the pores well, the excess was easy to clean off, and a few coats of white shellac sealed it permanently.

On July 11, 1928, I obtained a *brevet d'invention* for this method of decorating wood, which offered me "protection" against imitators until July 11, 1943. Unfortunately for me, this *brevet* contained a very detailed description of my method.

Although my shop had expanded to at least 10 times its original size and my work force averaged 25 to 30 people, I had a hard time coping with the incoming orders, not to mention pursuing the hundreds of people who, because of the description in the *brevet d'invention*, were imitating my process, first throughout France, then throughout Europe, and eventually throughout the world.

By this time my family had also increased, and I was glad to move into a comfortable and elegant penthouse apartment and enjoy a long-missed period of financial independence. The method of decoratively filling the pores of wood became a public science. By allowing this technique to become part of the public domain, I helped pave the way for a monumental breakthrough in wood finishing.

Colorless Color and Scorched Finish

One of the leaders in furniture design in France during the 1930s was Émile-Jacques Ruhlman. Though I disagree with the title "Master of Art Deco" bestowed upon him by many, there is no question that he was a designer who maintained the highest standards in cabinetmaking and never compromised on quality. On the drawing board, he was an artist who perfected the most elegant and harmonious lines. A Ruhlman-designed item can easily be recognized for its perfection in execution and elegance of design.

My feelings about Ruhlman are that though he achieved success, he did not accomplish his ultimate goal: the discovery of a revolutionary process in the woodworking field.

Ruhlman died the year I started my business. As my business expanded, many of his followers became my customers. Most of them continued his approach to design and tried to produce new and better-quality shapes and lines in the popular Art Deco style. Among my customers were Alix, Beaudoin, Boverie, Goldberg, Jallot, Jansen, Klotz, Laffaille, Levesque, Masse, Pascaud, Picard, and Sognot. I found myself working for the elite of the interior decorating trade, mostly on traditional, though routine, high-quality work.

Two immensely talented designers not content to follow the lead of Ruhlman, and with whom I worked, were Jean Pascaud and Maurice Laffaille. They were impressed by my new finishes and together we achieved several notable breakthroughs in the trade.

The two men were extremely different. Pascaud, at that time in his mid-thirties, was polished, formal, and reserved. He catered to international high society. He was a well-paying and serious customer. Maurice Laffaille, on the other hand, was an adventuresome, fun-loving person with whom I almost instantly became friends. He was closer in age to me than Pascaud.

I could say that Maurice and I worked together on these new finishes, but it is more accurate to say that he teased and challenged me into discovering them. During that period, we were installing two rooms in the country home of the Baron de Rothschild. I had the job of producing a finish for the two rooms. For one of the rooms, Maurice showed me a ball of twine and said: "George, look at this ball of twine! That's how you will finish the dining room of the Baron de Rothschild!"

The task I had, matching the finish of the dining room to the virgin hemp, seemed impossible since the virgin hemp had no color at all. Yet I succeeded in doing it!

The dining room was made of oak. To approach the colorless color of the virgin hemp, I cleaned the wood of all impurities with lye (see page 28). When the wood was physically and chemically clean, I bleached it with several applications of concentrated chlorine. Concentrated chlorine is easily available presently from suppliers of swimming-pool needs. Eau de Javelle was at the time the equivalent of the well-known American household bleach, Clorox®. It was also available in several degrees of concentration. With the help of this excellent bleach and the bright July sunshine, I came very close to matching my sample.

The protective coating of this unusual "colorless color" consisted of a thin coat of white shellac spiced, when nobody was looking, with a pinch of lithopone. (Lithopone is a white pigment that was popular years ago. Now, it is replaced by titanium dioxide.)

The Baron was absolutely enchanted when we installed this exceptional dining room in his chalet in Chantilly (Oise). Both Laffaille and I received great compliments as well as a case of his best champagne!

To this day, I don't think that such a finish was ever produced prior to this one by anyone, anywhere in the world. Without false modesty, I consider it a milestone in the history of the wood-finishing industry, one that was transformed by hard work, innovative techniques, and the support of decorators and clients alike into an *art*.

It must be noted that like many others who have discovered a revolutionary technique, I ran into unexpected problems. When the rainy October weather settled in, the concentrated chlorine stored in the pores of the wood attracted the air's moisture and the beautiful finish started to shed tears!

The chlorine had to be neutralized at once. To do this, I dissolved oxalic acid crystals in alcohol and applied this solution to the finish. The ensuing fumes were not the most pleasant, but the dining room stopped "weeping." It is probably still among the Baron's most cherished possessions.

The first lesson I learned from this experience was that chlorine bleach needs to be neutralized, and vinegar is a simple chemical to accomplish this. (On the Baron's dining room, I had to use an alcohol-soluble neutralizer to penetrate the shellac finish.) The second lesson I learned was that knowledge of chemistry seems to be the best road to superior and innovative wood finishing.

It took a week of hard work to restore the beauty of my colorless color finish. The lesson was difficult, but the Baron de Rothschild's dining-room set in Chantilly, France, remains as a testimonial to the breakthrough technique of colorless color, and has justified all my efforts.

When it came to tackling the Baron's bedroom, Maurice presented me with another equally challenging problem. Showing me a statue of the Buddha, Laffaille asked me to closely examine the texture and treatment of the hair. The Buddha's hair consisted of alternating lines of scorched and unscorched wood, each line about the size of a human hair. As of today it remains a mystery how anyone could scorch wood in such a delicate manner. I informed Maurice that even if I discovered the method for doing it, it would still take at least two thousand years to complete the entire bedroom. "You'll do it, George!" Maurice assured me. And he was right!

After weeks of exprimenting with different methods of scorching wood, I discovered that a plumber's blowtorch was the proper tool to use. Trying new approaches, I pointed its flame at a sample piece of pine selected for its beautiful markings. Slowly and steadily moving the flame back and forth, I scorched the sample until it became evenly black all over. This was a demanding process since I had to make sure while using the blowtorch that the heat applied would not ignite the wood. I turned off the blowtorch and proceeded to the next step, that of brushing off the loose particles from the wood. This messy operation needs to be done either outdoors or in a spray booth with a good exhaust fan working. I used a soft scrubbing brush, and with each stroke the unexpected beauty of the scorched wood was revealed. A subtle range of shades from virgin pine to charcoal black slowly appeared.

Another accomplishment was reached with the scorching of the wood. We wood finishers are generally concerned with the width and length of the area on which we are working. By scorching the sample and brushing off the loose particles, I revealed, or rather emphasized, the third dimension of the board: its thickness and texture. Prior to scorching, it had been a plain, flat board. After scorching and brushing, it was transformed into an attractive bas-relief landscape of high and low areas. The deep areas stayed close to the pine's natural color, while the high surfaces turned charcoal black. I emphasized this contrast with my handy tampon by coating the highlights with shellac and polishing them to a shiny black glow.

When the scorched bedroom set was delivered to the Baron de Rothschild's chalet in Chantilly, you can be sure that the Baron himself, Maurice Laffaille, and I were all jubilantly aware of the innovative artistry of this revolutionary technique. We realized that this finish was a milestone in the ever more sophisticated and demanding art of wood finishing.

Both Maurice and the Baron insisted that we apply for a patent for this method of finishing. While I have the original *brevet d'invention* concerning the decorative filling of pores, I cannot seem to locate the patent for this technique. It must be in the papers of either the Baron or Laffaille.

The *brevet d'invention* that I received in 1932 contained, once again, a detailed description of the scorching method. In 1939, at the World's Fair in Flushing, New York, four or five pavilions were presented that were made entirely of scorched pine; an additional four or five showed sections using such wood. It may have been a coincidence, but I often wonder.

Sandblasting

In 1935 or 1936, Jean Pascaud was commissioned to decorate the palace of the Pasha of Marrakech. Soon afterwards we met in conference, mostly to discuss one problem. The Pasha was a well-built, handsome man, the kind we call in French a *beau-mâle*. He was proud of his looks and virility. "Now," said Pascaud, "we need to match the furnishings of his bedroom to his personality." Pascaud further informed me that money was no object. However, even if he had told me that the job would not pay a *centime*, I would have tackled it with the same enthusiasm. It was a challenge I could not resist.

Two months and two hundred samples later, I produced an original finish that I feel any wood finisher since the beginning of the craft would be proud to say he discovered. This finish was used hand in hand with sandblasting.

Let's take a closer look at this particular achievement. The veneer used on the Pasha's ultraluxurious bedroom suite was quartered English oak, specially selected and flitch-matched. It was sawn to an eighth-of-an-inch (3 millimeters) thickness and was applied on the lumber core stock under a great amount of pressure. The shape of each item was utterly functional, straight, and simple. The quality of cabinet craft was the finest that experienced *ébénistes* could produce, and so would be the surface finish!

Though the wood was smooth and ready to be French-polished, that was not the plan we had in mind. Instead, we properly dismantled the bedroom suite in my atelier and then transferred it to my neighbor's premises. Omar Rapsaet was an excellent sculptor and glass engraver, and a master at handling a sandblaster. What he could accomplish by blasting various objects with sand propelled under enormous pressure borders on the incredible.

Just as I was never satisfied to be the second-best wood finisher in Paris, so Omar was the undisputed master of his profession. Masterfully, he sandblasted all the exposed parts of the oak bedroom suite.

Sandblasting is a technique that we often associate with Art Nouveau. We also think of it as a technique used primarily on glass to achieve that marvelous Lalique™ type of translucency. To my knowledge, it had never been used on wood until that time.

Sandblasting produces an endless repetition of "mountains" and "valleys." Though it seems easy, artistic sandblasting is really extremely difficult. It cannot be done on a large scale on the small machines marketed for the home craftsman. It takes far greater pressure than a home compressor can produce. When you use sand under pressure, you must protect yourself from head to toe and then pay great attention to the job you are doing. If you slow down for just a moment, you may go through the veneer or pierce an irreparable hole through the item.

After the bedroom suite was sandblasted, it was returned to me for the magic-finish treatment. I began by dyeing the bedroom suite pitch-black. Next, I dissolved alcohol-soluble black aniline dye, mixed it with my 250-gram shelliq and, using my best badger brush, applied two coats of the shellac evenly over all engraved areas.

It dried within a couple of hours. Only then did I begin the French polishing, of course not the traditional way. I made my tampon firmer than usual and fed it with smaller amounts of shelliq than usual. I did, however, cover the surfaces more frequently. Using blackened shelliq 250 and the open-pore finishing method, I coated all the "mountaintops" with a smooth, brilliant gloss. Sparing neither time nor effort, I did not stop until I achieved the decorative effect that I was aiming for. I covered all the "valleys" on the sandblasted wood with a uniform black veil, and crowned the "hills" with brilliant black snow.

The result was a finish that cannot be bought in the corner store nor found in any textbook. It was a custom finish that came straight from my heart. It started off as a soft *berceuse* or cradle song, gradually increasing in vibrant intensity until it became a song of the hills. It was what I considered the ultimate of finishes.

Commenting on my first book, *Adventures in Woodfinishing*, someone wrote that "this fellow George Frank did more for the woodworking industry than Hepplewhite, Sheraton, and Adams combined." When I first read this compliment, I shrugged my shoulders, shook my head, and smiled. Today, looking back on my accomplishments, and in particular on the finish I produced on the bedroom suite for the Pasha of Marrakech, I consider that statement in a different light.

Adams, Sheraton, Hepplewhite, and Ruhlman all created, produced, and perfected items made of wood. Their achievements were considerable. Yet their accomplishments centered around the design of the piece: shapes were harmonious and elegant, lines achieved through perfect execution, and decoration expressed through the use of decorative elements such as inlays, carvings, etc. Also, the problems they faced were the same as those encountered by the Pharaoh's woodworkers when, five thousand years ago, they were challenged to build a throne. Who is to say that the

The bedroom suite that I finished for the Pasha of Marrakech in the 1930s was probably the first time in the 5000-year history of furniture-making that elegant furniture was designed to emphasize the specially selected wood and the finish it was adorned with. Note the simple, box-like lines of this armoire designed exclusively for the new finish. This is a reproduction of the original photograph that appeared in a French magazine of that period.

solutions reached by the great masters of the trade of more recent times, such as the men mentioned above, were any better than those of woodworkers five thousand years past?

Prior to the 1930s, wood finishing had been considered an afterthought in woodworking. The designer of the piece had little use for the men who were responsible for its finish. The function of the piece, as well as general social tendencies, basically determined the shape and design of the item.

Suddenly I came along, bright-eyed and with a reverence and an understanding of the beauty of wrought wood. I spread my enthusiasm and appreciation of the possibilities of fascinating textures and finishes of the wood itself, and a new approach to cabinetmaking emerged. The decorators and designers began to consult me *before* designing and executing their pieces. Thus, I helped introduce a revolutionary new concept in the history of woodworking—the idea that the wood itself is a basic factor in determining the shape and design of the item being built.

Jean Pascaud, proud of the work done on the Marrakech palace, permitted the leading decorative art magazine, *Mobiliers et Décoration,* to publish an article on the job, well illustrated with photos. While he omitted mentioning my name as the originator of the finish, he did reveal that the wood had been sandblasted. This opened the door of imitation and opportunity for his competitors. He realized this too late.

As a result of the magazine article, Pascaud decided that all future work demanded secrecy. We began another bedroom suite for an unknown client. Pascaud never revealed that customer's name. He merely hinted that the husband was an abdicated British monarch, and the lady for whom the bedroom was being made was his wife, an American divorcee. It could only have been the Duke and Duchess of Windsor!

The wood for this bedroom was also oak. Oak comes in many varieties. This particular type had the closest, straightest grain to be found in oak. This plain, quarter-cut wood with straight vertical markings was also sandblasted by Omar Rapsaet. Once again he did a masterful job, and the engraving was uniform in depth throughout all areas.

Once Rapsaet had sandblasted the bedroom, my best friend and foreman of my shop, Ernest Vazsonyi, did the bleaching with hydrogen peroxide. To perform well, peroxide must be applied on top of an alkaline base. Ernest provided that base by soaking the wood surface with a fairly strong solution of lye—70–80 grams per liter (1000 grams) of water. He then sponged off all excess, and applied the hydrogen peroxide. It boiled, fumed, and dried white, but not white enough for me. The next day he repeated the operation; this time, the results were satisfactory.

There were also unexpected side benefits. Ernest, a rather handsome man, had curly hair that was a deep shade of chestnut. During the bleaching process, his hair, exposed over a period of time to liberated oxygen gases, developed blond streaks, much to the delight of his lady friends.

Ernest owned a black cat named Tom Tom who shadowed him everywhere. Tom Tom liked to supervise the bleaching process, and before long *his* hair also developed blond streaks, probably to the delight of the neighborhood female felines. I would not have been surprised if at that time hydrogen peroxide became a factor in the process of letting blondes have more fun.

Satisfied with the bleaching job, we neutralized the bleached surfaces by washing them with lots of clear water, and then sponging them off quickly so that the water would not have time to penetrate the wood. Thirty minutes later, the wood was dry, with no harm done. Still, as an added precaution, we let it dry overnight before applying a thin coat of pigmented shellac. This was plain, bleached shellac cut about 100 grams to a liter, into which we stirred some lithopone.

This shelliq was actually a thin shellac-paint, and since we did not have any spraying equipment, we used brushes. We covered the sandblasted areas with three applications of this thin paint, which dried into a flat, thin coating. Next, we smoothed the high points with fine sandpaper, first rubbing off the light paint from these areas and then French-polishing them with nonpigmented white shelliq. This created a subtle contrast between the flat valleys' very white areas, and the peaks, which although not very white became extremely shiny.

Pascaud then provided the final touch of elegance and artistry to the white bedroom suite, reviving the technique of *trompe l'oeil*. He painted a long black glove that seemed to just drape over the top drawer of the high chest. On the top of the low chest he painted a pair of canceled opera tickets, some loose change, and a key ring with keys. From five feet away, all these items looked perfectly real. They were painted with imagination and a great deal of talent prior to the final finish, and were well protected while the rest of the piece was being done.

The techniques described in this chapter all have one thing in common: They emphasize the three-dimensional nature of wood.

Wood, whatever its origin, color, and grain, is ready to accept hundreds of new finishes and to be beautified to degrees yet unknown. The limit is that of our creativity and artistic experimentation.

Whatever innovative and original effects I accomplished were the result of trying little-known ways with rarely tried products, using tools that now seem almost obsolete. I am really quite proud of these achievements. But the surface has just been scratched (pun intended!).

It is now time for *you*, dear reader, to face this exciting challenge. Only you can finish the job I started—that of elevating wood finishing to the skill, science, and art it deserves to be.

Editor's Note on Safety

Following is a list of the chemicals most commonly used and the potential dangers they pose:

Tannic acid is the most basic ingredient in chemical staining. In woods like oak, walnut, and mahogany, the tannic acid or tannin is already present in the wood. Woods that are low in tannin require an application of tannic acid before some of the chemical stains will be effective. To make a solution for this purpose, mix five parts tannic acid with 95 parts water. Apply the solution to the work and let it dry before applying any other chemicals. *Tannic acid is toxic when eaten or inhaled.*

Ammonia reacts with tannin to produce a wide range of brown colors. Industrial-strength ammonia produces the best results, but household ammonia can be used. It can be applied as a liquid or used in the fuming process. Ammonia has an advantage over other alkalis, because it completely evaporates from the wood. Other alkalis leave a residue that must be neutralized. *Breathing the concentrated fumes of ammonia may be fatal, so always provide adequate ventilation. There is a moderate fire danger if ammonia fumes reach a point of 16 to 25 percent of the atmosphere.*

Potash (potassium carbonate) produces results similar to ammonia. It comes as a powder that must be dissolved in water before use. It leaves a residue on the wood after it has dried. To remove the residue, wash with clean water and then neutralize it with a wash of household vinegar. Finally, wash with clean water again. *Potash is a skin irritant.*

Caustic soda (sodium hydroxide) is similar to potash in effect and must be neutralized in the same manner. *Caustic soda will burn the skin and is poisonous if swallowed.*

Potassium permanganate produces a wide range of beautiful browns when applied to high-tannin woods or over a wash of tannic acid. It comes in crystal form. Dissolve 1½ ounces of crystals into one quart of water for a medium brown. The solution will first turn the wood violet, but the color will change to brown as the wood dries. Potassium permanganate should always be used in a diluted solution; *this chemical may cause burns, and strong solutions can pose a fire risk.*

Potassium dichromate is similar to potassium permanganate except that the color produced tends to be more yellowish. *This chemical is poisonous if inhaled or swallowed. It may cause skin burns, and strong solutions can pose a fire risk.*

Copper sulfate also produces a gray or black color when applied to wood. *It is poisonous if swallowed.*

Glossary

The chemicals and products listed here are defined only according to their uses in wood finishing. Also, terms that follow in parentheses are other names the chemicals and products are known by.

Acacia (Arabic gum) A light glue that serves as a binder.

Acetone A paint, varnish, and lacquer solvent.

Alcanet root Used to convey a red tint to oil.

Alcohol Only Completely Denatured Alcohol (CDA) is allowed to be used in wood finishing, as a solvent for spirit varnishes.

Alum (correct name, aluminum potassium sulphate) An excellent mordant.

Ammonia A gas that is usually dissolved in water. It darkens wood that contains tannic acid.

Aqua fortis *See* Nitric acid.

Archil *See* Orchil.

Asphaltum A petroleum by-product that is used with fillers as a colorant and a binder.

Baking soda *See* Soda bicarbonate.

Benzoin (correct name, benzoin resin or gum benzoin) An additive to spirit varnish that improves its gloss.

Bimsstein German name for a polishing compound, the main ingredient of which is pumice stone.

Binder The part of the paint that holds the pigment particles together. It is the "heart" of the coating.

Bitumen *See* Asphaltum.

Bluestone (blue vitriol) *See* Copper sulphate.

Borax An excellent cleaner.

Brazilwood extract A dye—used for the last 500 years—which, when combined with various mordants, produces a variety of red colors.

Brimstone Sulfur.

Calcium chloride Used in varnish for musical instruments.

Camphor (gum camphor) When dissolved in alcohol, it adds an interesting scent to alcohol varnishes.

Camphorated oil Used as a fragrance.

Candelilla wax A hard vegetable wax most often used mixed with other, softer waxes.

Carborundum Trademark name that refers to various abrasives.

Carnauba wax The hardest of all waxes, used mixed with softer ones.

Catalyst A chemical that initiates reactions in other chemicals.

Catechu plant Its extract, when combined with mordants, is used as a dye.

Caustic soda *See* Sodium hydroxide.

Ceresin wax A refined ozokerite, this mineral wax is most often used combined with other waxes.

Chalk (calcium carbonate) Is mostly used in fillers or as a pigment.

Chlorine of lime *See* Lime.

Chrome *See* Potassium dichromate.

Citronellal A lemon-scented industrial fragrance.

Cochineal An insect that produced the most popular red dye before the advent of synthetic dyes.

Copal A fossil resin used in varnishes.

Copper sulphate (cupric sulphate, blue vitriol, or bluestone) A crystal that has many uses, such as a wood preservative and/or a mordant.

Cream of tartar (proper name, potassium bitartrate) Baking product that is used as a mordant.

Cutch extract An old-time dye that must be combined with mordants.

Dextrin An adhesive that is used as a binder.

Dragon's blood A resin used as a pigment in paints and lacquers.

Emery powder (carborundum) An abrasive that is the natural form of aluminum oxide.

Ethanol (ethyl alcohol or grain alcohol) Unlawful to use in finishing.

Eucalyptus oil Used as a fragrance.

Ferric acetate Used as a wood preservative and also as a mordant.

Formaldehyde A water-soluble gas used mostly as a disinfectant and also as a preservative.

Fustic dye An old-time, nature-produced dye.

Gallnuts *See* Nutgall.

Gelatin An animal product used as a binder or light glue.

Gesso A paint composed of chalk (pigment), water (carrier), and rabbit-skin glue (binder).

Glauber's salt (sodium sulphate) Is used as a mordant.

Glycerin (glycerol) A trihydroxy alcohol and a versatile chemical. It is used when gilding.

Hydrated lime (slaked lime) Used in antique reproductions.

Hydrochloric acid (muriatic acid) Used to fade colors in antique reproductions.

Hydrogen peroxide The most powerful bleach used in wood finishing, when combined with lye or other alkalines.

Hypo Common term for sodium thiosulphate. It is used in combination with potassium permanganate, as a bleach.

Indigo Dyestuff found in approximately 200 plants. Now, it is manufactured synthetically.

Iron (ferrous sulphate, iron vitriol, or copperas) Is used as a mordant and also as a wood preservative.

Javel (Javelle) French equivalent of the American bleach Clorox®.

Lac dye Blood-red dye that is extracted from the same insect that produces the shellac.

Lanolin Grease, extracted from wool, that is used to protect the finisher's hands.

Latex Rubber-related chemical used as a binder in water-based (emulsion) paints.

Lime (calcium oxide) Readily absorbs water. It is used "slacked" to create antique finishes.

Linseed oil, boiled Actually, there is no such thing, since the oil does not boil. Drier is added to the heated oil, which induces it to dry faster.

Litharge A yellow pigment used in varnishes and paints.

Lithopone An excellent white pigment, now replaced by titanium dioxide.

Lye *See* Sodium hydroxide.

Madder root One of the earliest used dyes. It is now replaced with synthetic alizarin.

Mandrake A root alleged to have many supernatural qualities or properties. Yellow dye can be produced from it.

Mineral oil (paraffin oil) A petroleum distillate used in French polishing and in polishes in general.

Mordants Chemicals that fix dyes in materials.

Naphtha A petroleum distillate used as a solvent.

Nitric acid (aqua fortis) Used to age wood and metal.

Nutgall Nutlike, insect-induced growth on wild oak trees. Its brew is rich in tannic acid and is used as a mordant.

Oil of vitriol Obsolete term for sulfuric acid.

Orchil (orseille) A lichen that yields a violet dye.

Oxalic acid Crystals which, when dissolved in water, are frequently used for bleaching.

Paraffin oil *See* Mineral oil.

Paraffin wax A petroleum by-product, most often used mixed with other waxes.

Paraloid B-72 Trade name for a disinfectant used in museums to disinfect antiques.

Pearl ash *See* Potash.

Peroxide *See* Hydrogen peroxide.

Picric acid Solution of crystals that is used mostly in antique reproductions.

Plaster of Paris (proper name, calcium sulphate) Used as a binder for filler.

Potash (pearl ash) Actually potassium carbonate. It is used primarily as a mordant.

Potassium dichromate (or bichromate) A well-known, widely used mordant.

Potassium hydroxide (sodium hydroxide, caustic soda, or lye) *See* Sodium hydroxide.

Potassium permanganate Years ago, was used as a bleach when combined with hypo.

Pumice Well-known volcanic stone that is an excellent abrasive.

Pyrogallic acid (pyrogallol) Mordant used to produce the "perfect" black.

Rosin Resin derived from pine trees that is used in varnishes and as a binder in some fillers.

Rottenstone Fine abrasive that is also used to imitate dust.

Safflower Herb known as far back as 2000 B.C. that yields yellow-to-red dyes.

Sal soda (sodium carbonate decahydrate) Used mostly for cleaning, as a detergent.

Sandarac Resin used in alcohol varnishes and in lacquers.

Soda bicarbonate (sodium bicarbonate) Simple baking soda. It makes a good mordant which, when combined with dyes, produces interesting colors (such as shades of blues).

Sodium hydroxide (caustic soda or lye) The most important chemical, used primarily in antique reproduction or aging wood.

Sodium hypochlorite Better known as Clorox® bleach.

Sour water (commercial vitriol) Diluted sulfuric acid.

Talc (talcum powder or soapstone) A soft mineral that is used by wood finishers mostly in fillers.

Tannic acid A chemical in many various forms, and one of the more widely used mordants which can be dissolved in water, alcohol, and acetone.

Tin crystals (stannous chloride) One of the oldest mordants, it was used as far back as 5000 years ago.

Triethanolamine An emulsifier chemical.

Tripoli earth A very fine abrasive that also absorbs oil.

Trisodium phosphate An excellent cleaner used to clean old brushes, etc.

Vinegar Used as a mordant and also as a neutralizer.

Vitriol (oil of vitriol) Sulfuric acid or, frequently, its very diluted variation.

White copperas Sulphate of zinc. It is used as a mordant.

Whiting Powdered chalk, used as a mild abrasive and in fillers.

METRIC EQUIVALENCY CHART

Length

UNIT	ABBREVIATION	*Number of Metres*	APPROXIMATE U.S. EQUIVALENT
myriametre	mym	10,000	6.2 miles
kilometre	km	1000	0.62 mile
hectometre	hm	100	109.36 yards
dekametre	dam	10	32.81 feet
metre	m	1	39.37 inches
decimetre	dm	0.1	3.94 inches
centimetre	cm	0.01	0.39 inch
millimetre	mm	0.001	0.04 inch

Area

UNIT	ABBREVIATION	*Number of Square Metres*	APPROXIMATE U.S. EQUIVALENT
square kilometre	sq km *or* km^2	1,000,000	0.3861 square miles
hectare	ha	10,000	2.47 acres
are	a	100	119.60 square yards
centare	ca	1	10.76 square feet
square centimetre	sq cm *or* cm^2	0.0001	0.155 square inch

Volume

UNIT	ABBREVIATION	*Number of Cubic Metres*	APPROXIMATE U.S. EQUIVALENT
dekastere	das	10	13.10 cubic yards
stere	s	1	1.31 cubic yards
decistere	ds	0.10	3.53 cubic feet
cubic centimetre	cu cm *or* cm^3 *also* cc	0.000001	0.061 cubic inch

Capacity

UNIT	ABBREVIATION	*Number of Litres*	*Cubic*	*Dry*	*Liquid*
kilolitre	kl	1000	1.31 cubic yards		
hectolitre	hl	100	3.53 cubic feet	2.84 bushels	
dekalitre	dal	10	0.35 cubic foot	1.14 pecks	2.64 gallons
litre	l	1	61.02 cubic inches	0.908 quart	1.057 quarts
decilitre	dl	0.10	6.1 cubic inches	0.18 pint	0.21 pint
centilitre	cl	0.01	0.6 cubic inch		0.338 fluidounce
millilitre	ml	0.001	0.06 cubic inch		0.27 fluidram

Mass and Weight

UNIT	ABBREVIATION	*Number of Grams*	APPROXIMATE U.S. EQUIVALENT
metric ton	MT *or* t	1,000,000	1.1 tons
quintal	q	100,000	220.46 pounds
kilogram	kg	1,000	2.2046 pounds
hectogram	hg	100	3.527 ounces
dekagram	dag	10	0.353 ounce
gram	g *or* gm	1	0.035 ounce
decigram	dg	0.10	1.543 grains
centigram	cg	0.01	0.154 grain
milligram	mg	0.001	0.015 grain

Index

Numbers in italics refer to color section.